9-10

DATE DUE

AUG 2 6 2014		
DEC 3 0 2014		
MAY 1 9 2015		
JUN 1 6 2015		
OCT 0 3 2015		
OCT 1 3 2015		
OCT 1 8 2018		
SEP 2 3 2022		
		PRINTED IN U.S.A.

This library edition published in 2011 by Walter Foster Publishing, Inc.
Walter Foster Library
Distributed by Black Rabbit Books.
P.O. Box 3263 Mankato, Minnesota 56002

Printed in China by PRINTPLUS Limited, Shenzhen.

First Library Edition

Library of Congress Cataloging-in-Publication Data

Farrell, Russell.
  All about drawing sea creatures & animals / illustrated by Russell Farrell
and Diana Fisher. -- 1st library ed.
      p. cm.
  ISBN 978-1-936309-08-5 (hardcover)
  1. Marine animals in art--Juvenile literature. 2. Drawing--Technique--
Juvenile literature. I. Fisher, Diana. II. Title.
  NC781.F365 2011
  743.6--dc22

                                                        2010004212

022010
OP1808

9 8 7 6 5 4 3 2 1

All About
DRAWING

Sea Creatures & Animals

Illustrated by Russell Farrell and Diana Fisher

Getting Started

When you **look** closely at the **drawings** in this book, you'll notice that they're made up of basic shapes, such as circles, triangles, and rectangles. To draw all your underwater and wild kingdom favorites, just start with simple shapes as you see here. It's easy and fun!

Circles

are used to draw eyes, heads, and round bodies.

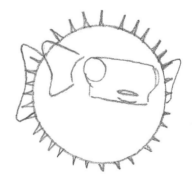

Ovals
are good for drawing animals' bodies.

Triangles
are best for drawing the heads of some fish.

FIND THE SHAPE!

Can you find a circle, an oval, and a triangle on this colorful toucan? Look closely at the beak, eye, and body. It's easy to see the basic shapes in any animal once you know what to look for!

Coloring Tips

There's more than one way to bring your **animal** friends to life on paper—you can use crayons, markers, or colored pencils. Just be sure you have plenty of good natural colors—blue, green, and brown, plus gray, yellow and orange.

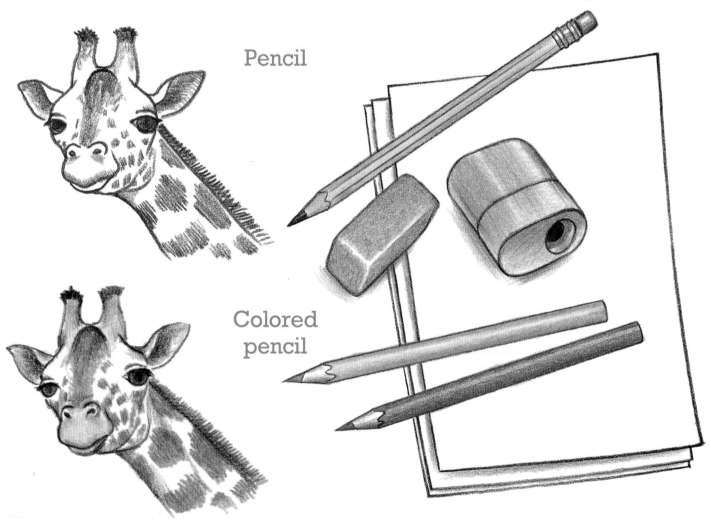

Pencil

Colored pencil

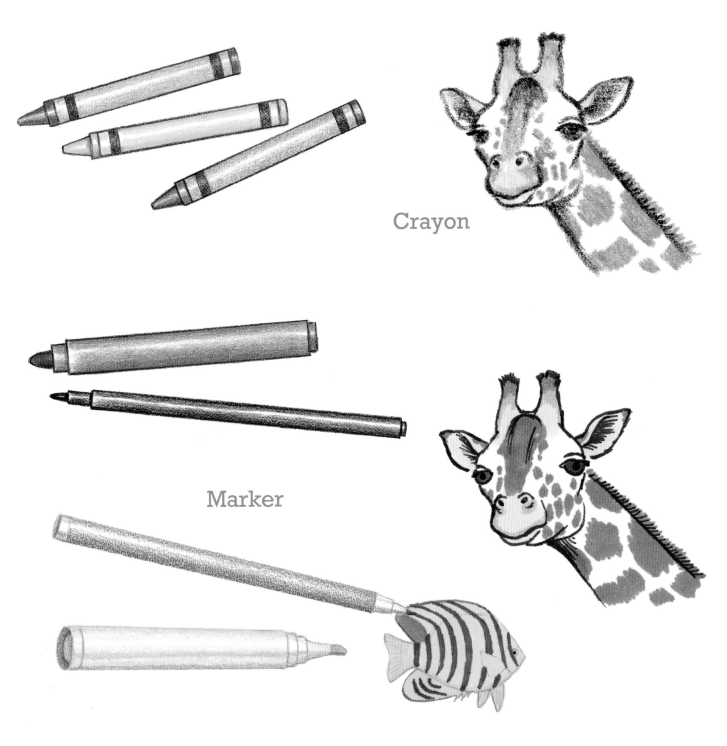

Crayon

Marker

FUN TIP!

With an assortment of creatures under the sea and on land, the color possibilities are endless! Before you pick a coloring tool for your drawing, think about the animal's different textures. Is its skin furry, feathered, scaled, or smooth? Colored pencils have a sharp tip that is great for tiny details like small hairs and feathers. Crayons can be used to cover large areas quickly and markers make your colors look smooth and solid.

Puffer

The body of the **puffer** is one of the **simplest** shapes of all sea creatures—its body is nearly a perfect circle!

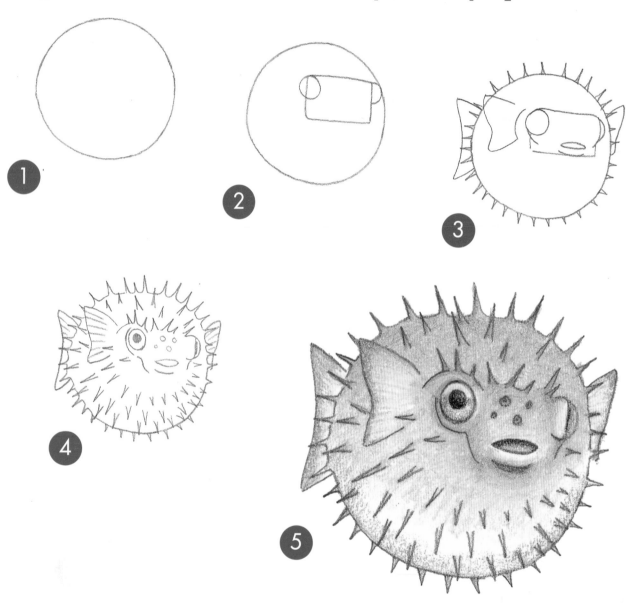

With all the predators in the ocean, many fish have adapted unique ways to defend themselves. The puffer (also called the "blowfish" or "swellfish") can fill itself up with air or water to become a round, spiky ball, making it very difficult to swallow!

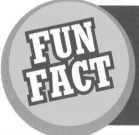

Aardvark

The aardvark has a **long** nose, **beady** eyes, and sharp claws. It first smells and then digs out its meals of ants and termites.

1

2

3

4

5

LOW RISK!

There are many aardvarks in the world today, so this animal is at low risk for extinction. *Extinct* means that none are left.

6

Angelfish

An **elegant** creature, this **tropical** fish is known for its vibrant stripes of color.

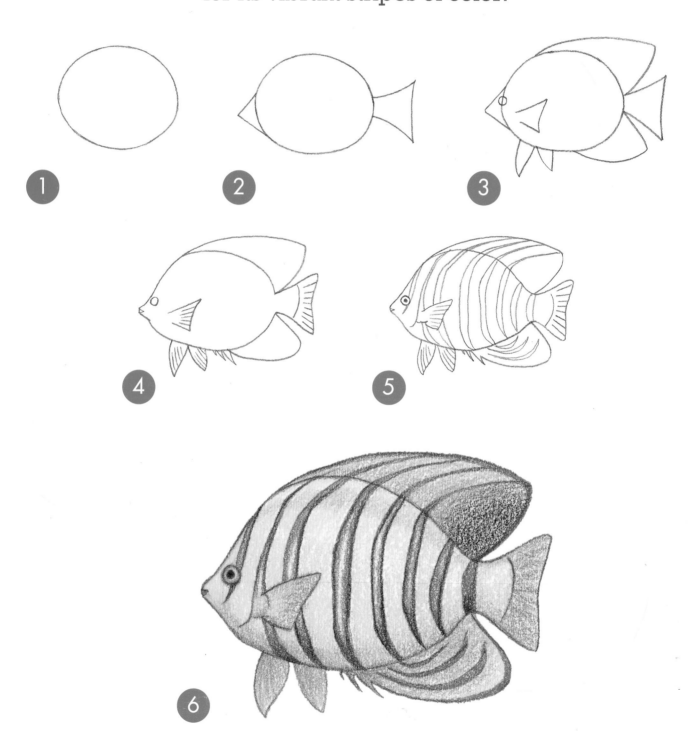

1

2

3

4

5

6

Emu

The emu's **fluffy** plumage hides its small **wings.** But its tall, thin legs allow this flightless bird to run up to 30 miles per hour!

FUN FACT

Some say the emu's name comes from Arabic or Aboriginal words for "large bird"; others say it mimics the male bird's call of "e-moo."

Giant Panda

In China the **barrel-shaped** panda is called "baixiong" ("white bear"), but the black markings give this animal a two-toned look.

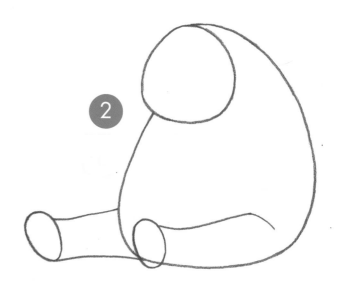

FUN FACT

The giant panda has a very limited diet—it survives almost entirely on bamboo! It eats the shoots of this grasslike plant in the spring, the leaves in the summer, and the stems in the winter.

Polar Bear

The cuddly polar bear has a **large,** round, **furry** body—but this cutie hunts and devours seals, walruses, and even whales!

5

SO COOL!

Polar bears are so well insulated that sometimes they overheat and have to cool off in the icy water! They also spend a lot of time bathing after meals to keep their thick coats white fur clean.

Harp Seal

Draw this **sweet** baby harp seal with **rounded,** gently curving lines and big, dark, "puppy-dog" eyes.

FUN FACT

A baby harp seal is born with thick white fur, but after 1-1/2 weeks it develops a gray-brown coat with darker, harp-shaped (or horseshoelike) patches.

Toucan

keel-billed

It's hard to ignore the **keel-billed** toucan's beak! It's almost as long as the bird's body—and it features a rainbow of colors.

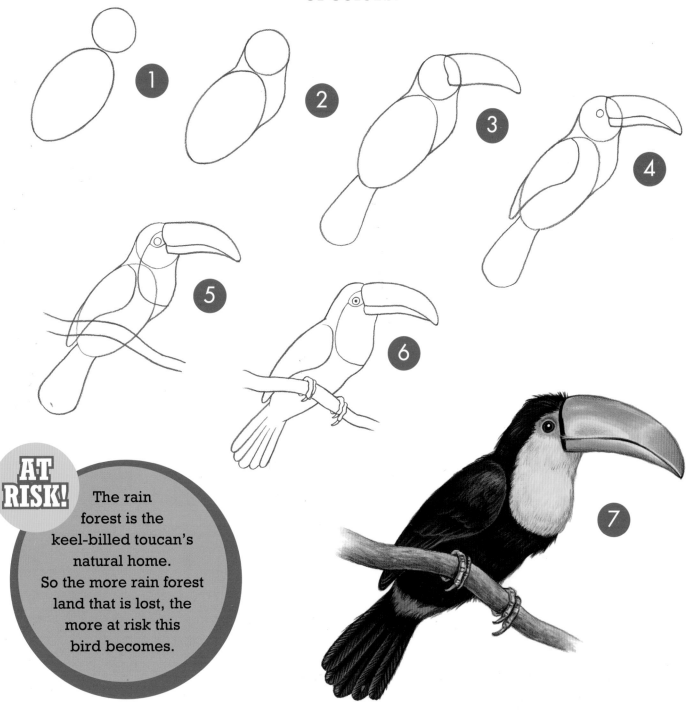

AT RISK! The rain forest is the keel-billed toucan's natural home. So the more rain forest land that is lost, the more at risk this bird becomes.

Cheetah

With its **long,** powerful legs; **lean,** muscular body; and stylish, spotted coat, you might say the cheetah is a hunter that's "dressed to kill"!

CALL OF THE JUNGLE

Unlike lions and tigers, cheetahs don't roar, but they do purr, growl, bark, and even make chirruping sounds!

5

6

Reaching speeds of more than 60 mph, the cheetah is the fastest animal in the world, but this big cat can maintain its top speed only for short bursts. After 10–12 seconds of running, the cheetah begins to overheat.

Humpback Whale

Weighing in at **2 tons,** the humpback is a **whale** of a creature—its huge fins are nearly 1/3 as long as its body!

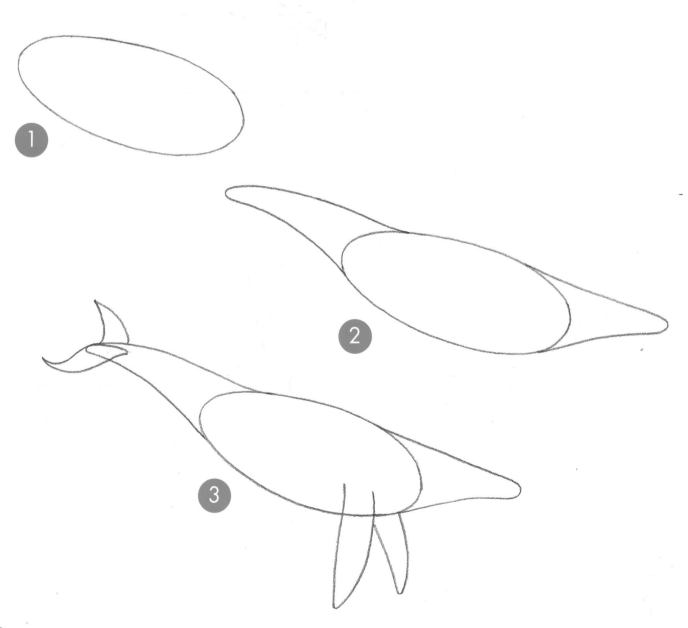

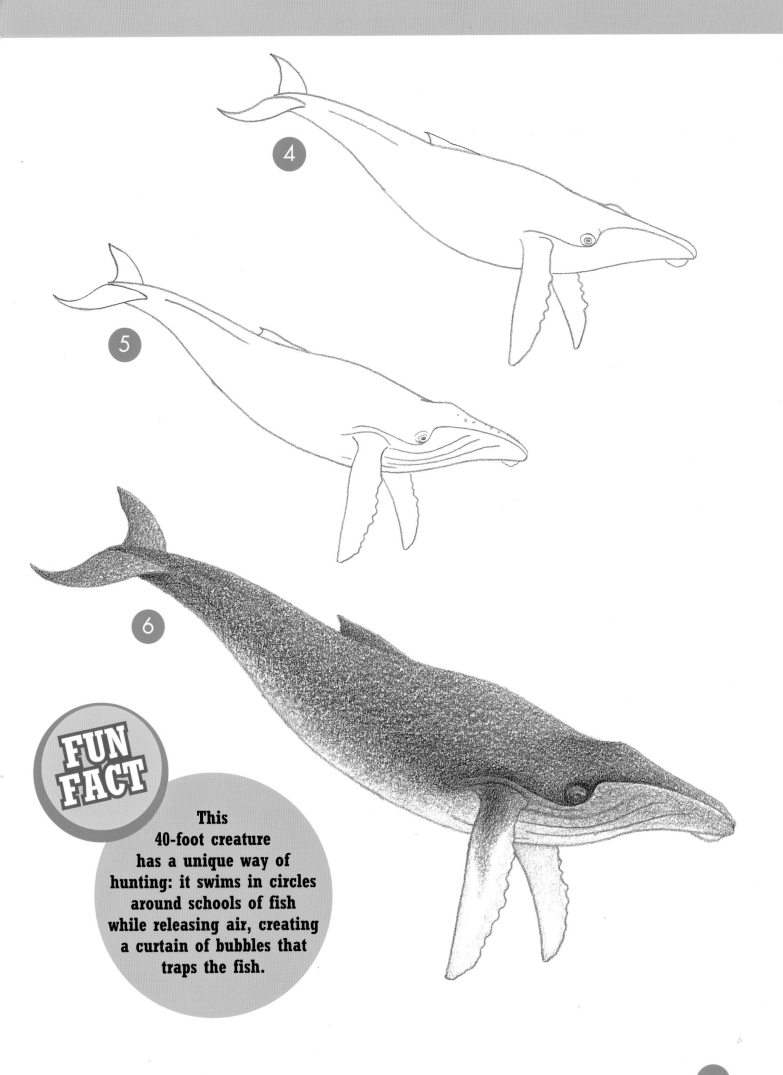

FUN FACT

This 40-foot creature has a unique way of hunting: it swims in circles around schools of fish while releasing air, creating a curtain of bubbles that traps the fish.

Sea Star

Start drawing this **sea** animal with simple **circles!**
Then add five triangular arms to create the star shape.

1

2

3

4

5

Wildebeest

The wildebeest—or gnu—looks **big** and **broad** with high shoulders and a humped back, but it prances away from danger on four skinny legs!

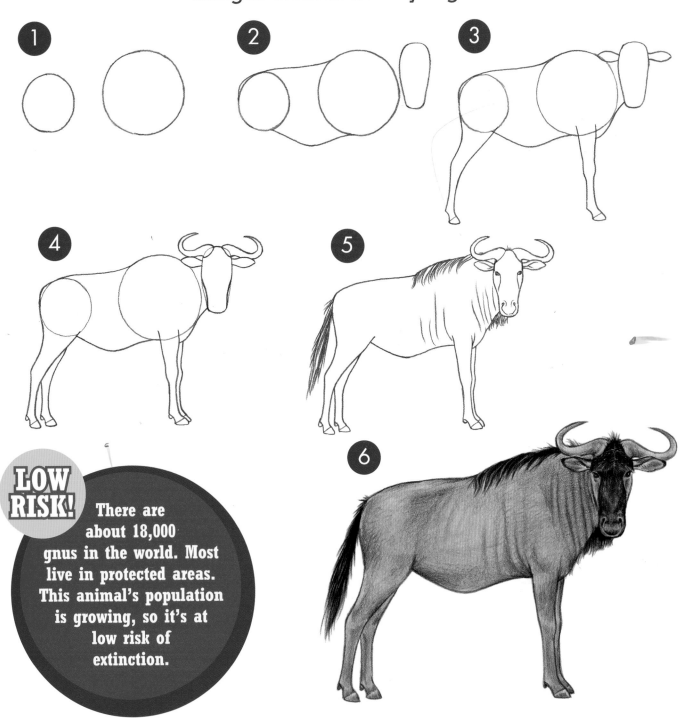

1

2

3

4

5

6

LOW RISK! There are about 18,000 gnus in the world. Most live in protected areas. This animal's population is growing, so it's at low risk of extinction.

Elephant

One of the largest beasts of the animal kingdom,
an African elephant has a thick trunk, big legs, long tusks,
and giant ears!

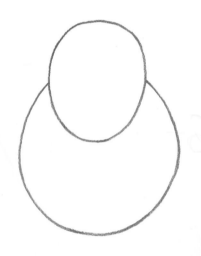

1

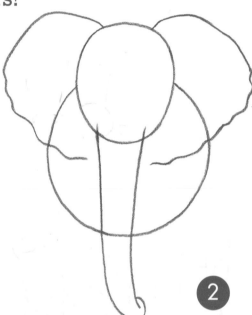

2

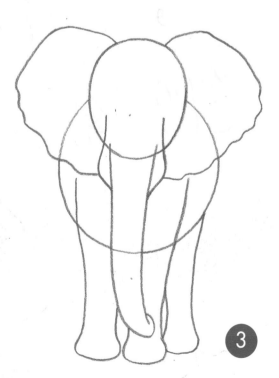

3

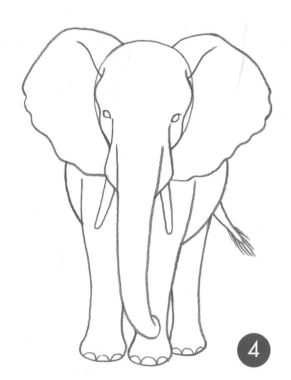

4

5

The elephant is known for its great memory—but why? One reason is the elephant has an enormous brain! Weighing in at around 12 pounds, it's the largest and heaviest mammal brain. (The human brain weighs only about 3 pounds.)

6

Great White Shark

The most **feared** of all sharks, this **predator** has a long, pointed snout and razor-sharp, triangular teeth.

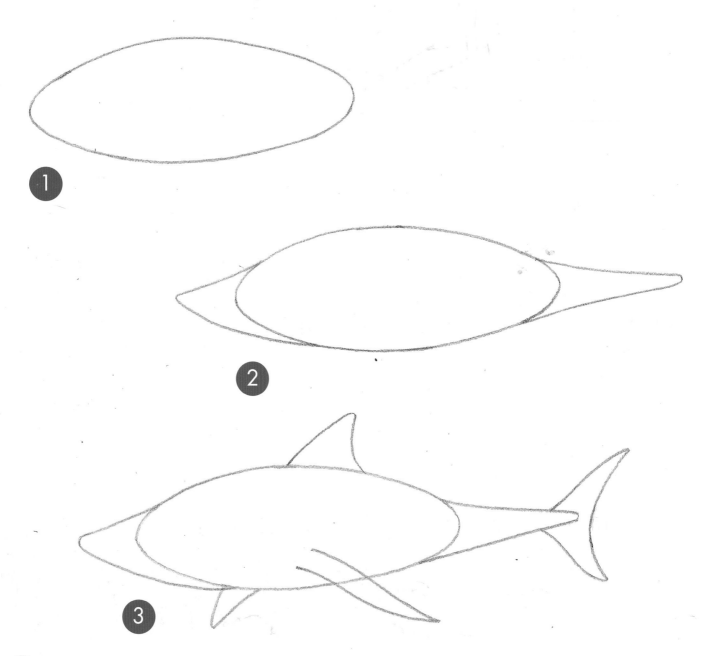

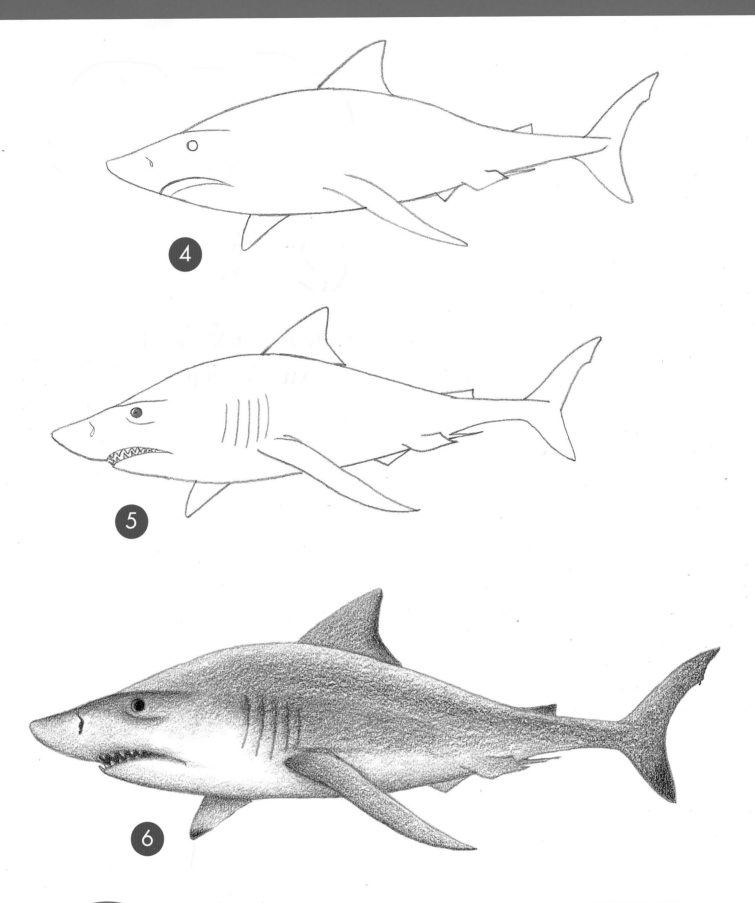

4

5

6

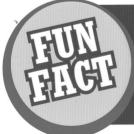

Incredibly, a great white has about 3,000 jagged teeth, which are arranged in several rows. The shark uses only the first two rows for capturing prey; the rest of the teeth move into position when the front teeth are damaged or fall out.

Crocodile

Start with a thin **oval** body and a small **round** head—
then add the crocodile's long, strong tail and big, powerful jaws!

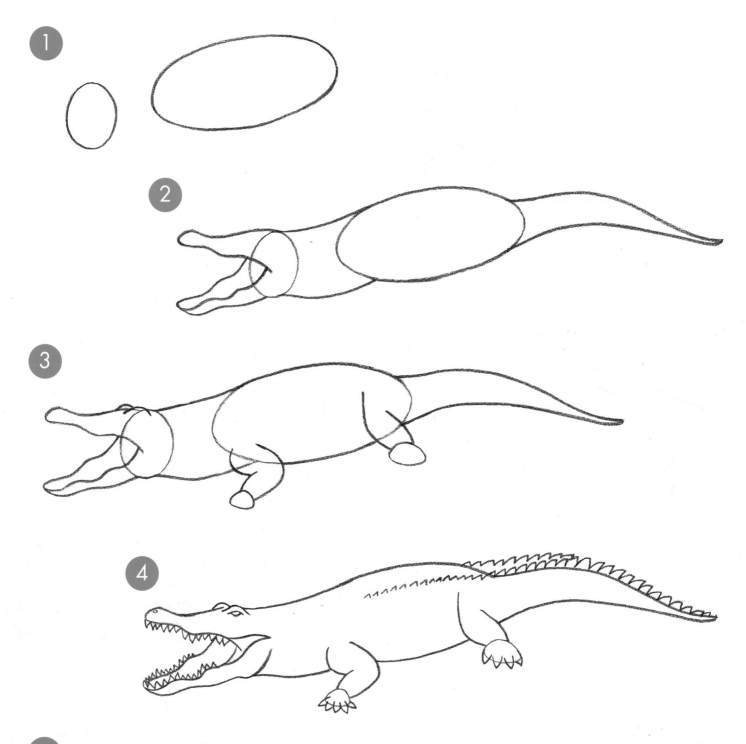

1

2

3

4

5

6

Sea Otter

This **cute** critter has **webbed** back feet, tiny ears, a foot-long tail, and thick brown fur.

Tiger

Every **big cat** has a large head and rounded ears. But a tiger also has *camouflaging* stripes that help this stand-out cat blend in!

Clownfish

A popular saltwater aquarium creature, the eye-catching clownfish sports bright gold bands of color.

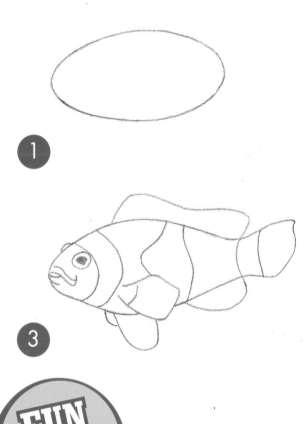

1

2

3

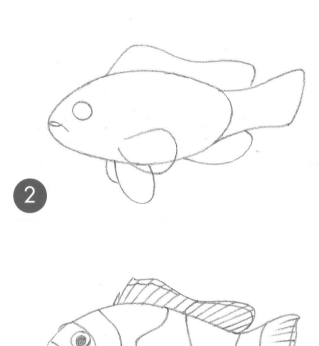

4

FUN FACT

The clownfish and sea anemone (an animal on the seafloor that resembles a flower) depend on one another for survival. After the anemone catches and eats a fish, the clownfish gets the leftovers that float nearby. In return, the clownfish protects the anemone from predators.

5

Lemur

Although its **long,** curving tail is the **ring-tailed** lemur's most striking feature, this animal is also known for its graceful, catlike posture.

GIRLS RULE!

In the ring-tailed lemur world, girls rule! Lemurs live in groups of 5–25, each with a few females in charge. Young females stay with the group, but young males must move to another group when they are still young.

Giraffe

With its lanky legs and long neck, the towering giraffe rises to claim the title of "tallest animal on Earth."

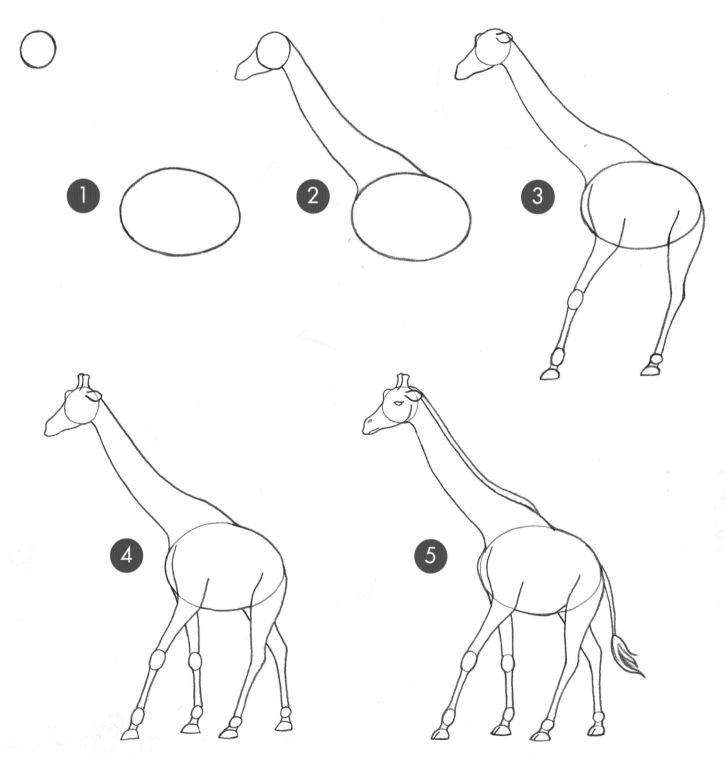

FUN FACT

A baby giraffe, called a "calf," can stand up on its own about 20 minutes after it's born! And, at birth, a giraffe calf already measures about 6-1/2 feet tall!

Dolphin

A **playful,** intelligent animal, the **dolphin** has a bottle-shaped beak and a happy expression that shows its friendly nature.

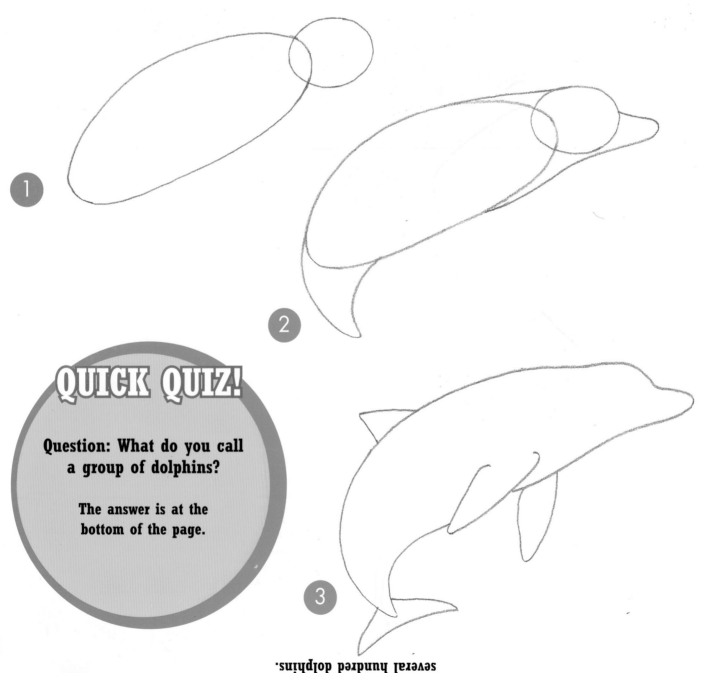

1

2

QUICK QUIZ!

Question: What do you call a group of dolphins?

The answer is at the bottom of the page.

3

Quick Quiz Answer: A pod. Sometimes these social creatures live in pods of up to several hundred dolphins.

4

5

FUN FACT

If you ever see a dolphin with just one eye open, chances are it's just sleeping! Because a dolphin can stay underwater for only 10 minutes before returning to the surface for air, it has to remain somewhat awake at all times. As a result, only one-half of the brain—and one eye—sleeps at one time!

Komodo

Don't let its **draggin'** belly fool you—the **large,** wrinkled, prehistoric-looking Komodo dragon is a swift runner and a fast climber.

Armadillo

Oddly enough, the "nine-banded" armadillo can have from 8 to 10 bands around its body, making its tough armor more flexible.

1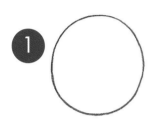

2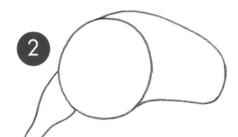

3

4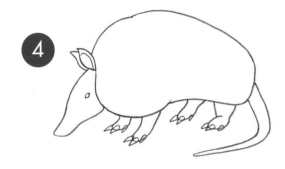

Many mammals give birth to multiple young, but only the nine-banded armadillo regularly produces them all from a single egg. The female always gives birth to quadruplets—that's four identical baby armadillos!

FOUR OF A KIND

5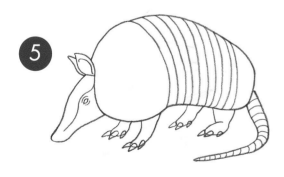

6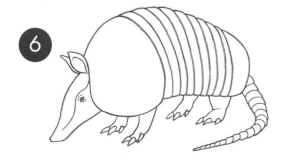

7

Sea Turtle

Begin drawing this **shelled** sea **creature** using a small circle for the head and an egg shape for the body.

FUN FACT

Sea turtles can feel vibrations in the water. This can help them locate food or steer clear of predators. They also have an excellent sense of smell.

SWELL SHELL

Contrary to what you may see in cartoons, a turtle can't crawl out of its shell, because the shell is part of its skeleton. Land turtles can pull their heads and limbs under their shells for protection, whereas sea turtles have streamlined shells and long, paddle-like flippers for faster swimming.

Animals in the Wild

Each animal has a **natural environment,** or *habitat*—whether a desert, forest, or water. To realistically portray your favorite animals, draw them in their own wild habitat, like this African grassland!

Underwater World

After you've learned to draw all the **fascinating** creatures in this book, try creating an awesome underwater scene!

Hippopotamus

"Massive" is a good start for describing this round, hulking beast! A full-grown hippo can weigh up to 1-1/2 tons.

LOW RISK!

The hippopotamus is plentiful in the African wild. Its population numbers are steady, so it has a low risk of becoming extinct.

7

8

9

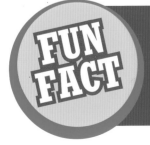

Stingray

A bottom-dweller, the stingray has a thin, flat body that allows it to both hide in the sand and glide through the water.

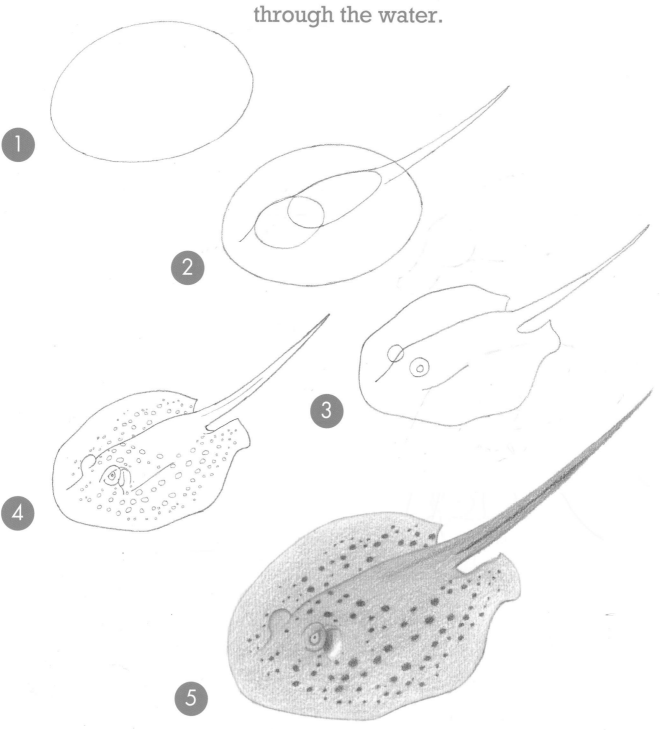

Platypus
duck's bill

It may have a **duck's bill** and webbed feet, but the platypus's flat tail and velvety, waterproof coat are all its own!

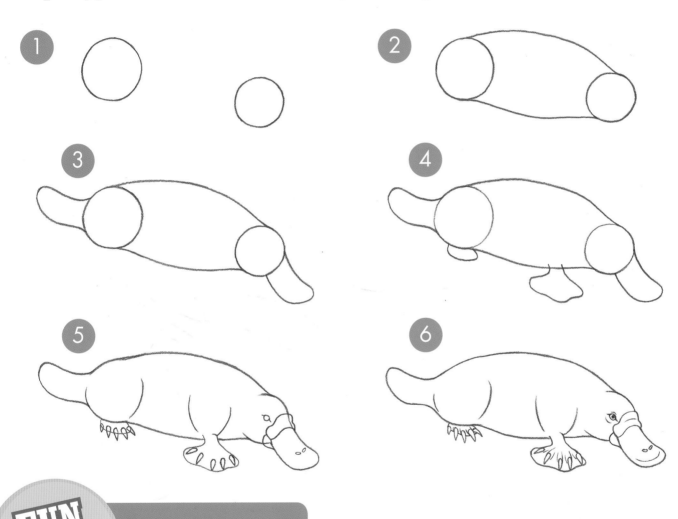

1

2

3

4

5

6

7

FUN FACT

The platypus isn't psychic, but it does have ESP—extra sensory perception! In addition to using sight, sound, taste, smell, and touch, the platypus can sense electrical signals with its snout, helping it find food underwater.

Kangaroo

With a **thick,** powerful tail, **strong** hind legs, and huge rear feet, you can identify the kangaroo from a hop, skip, and a jump away!

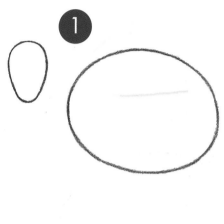

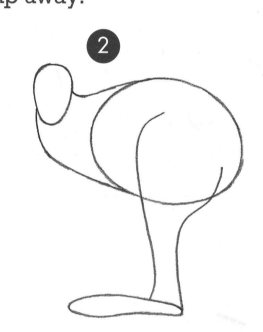

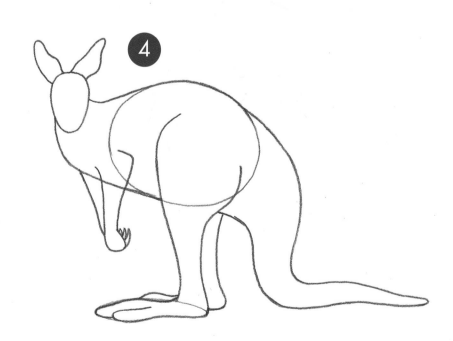

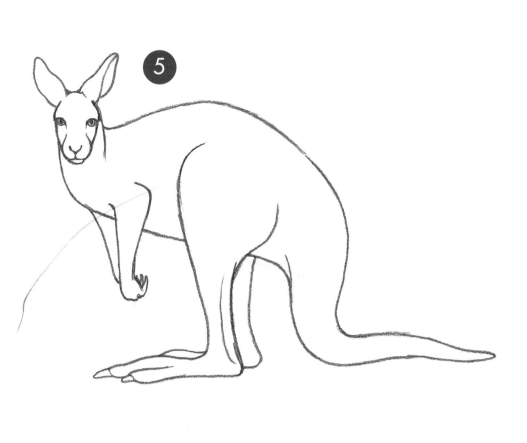

5

6

Walrus

The walrus is known for its **big, blubbery** body and its huge tusks, which can be up to 3 feet long!

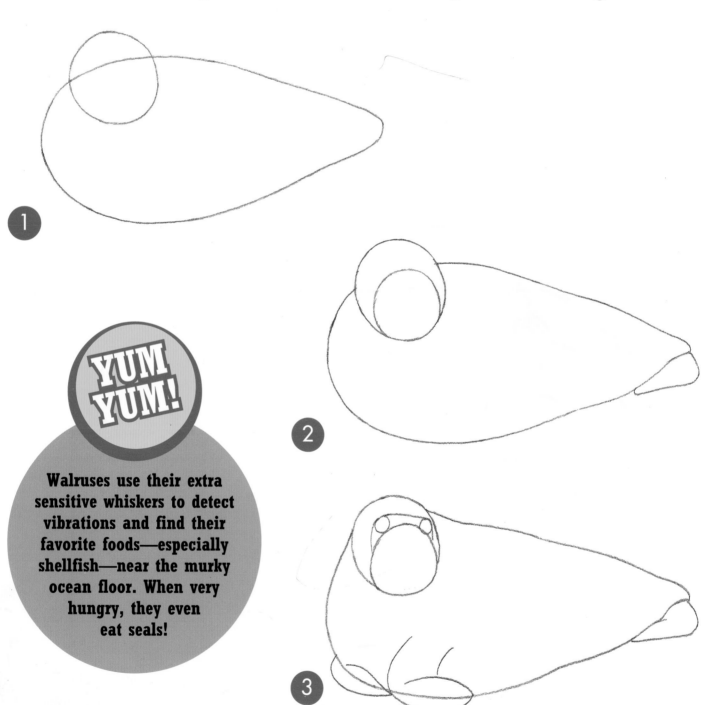

YUM YUM!

Walruses use their extra sensitive whiskers to detect vibrations and find their favorite foods—especially shellfish—near the murky ocean floor. When very hungry, they even eat seals!

1

2

3

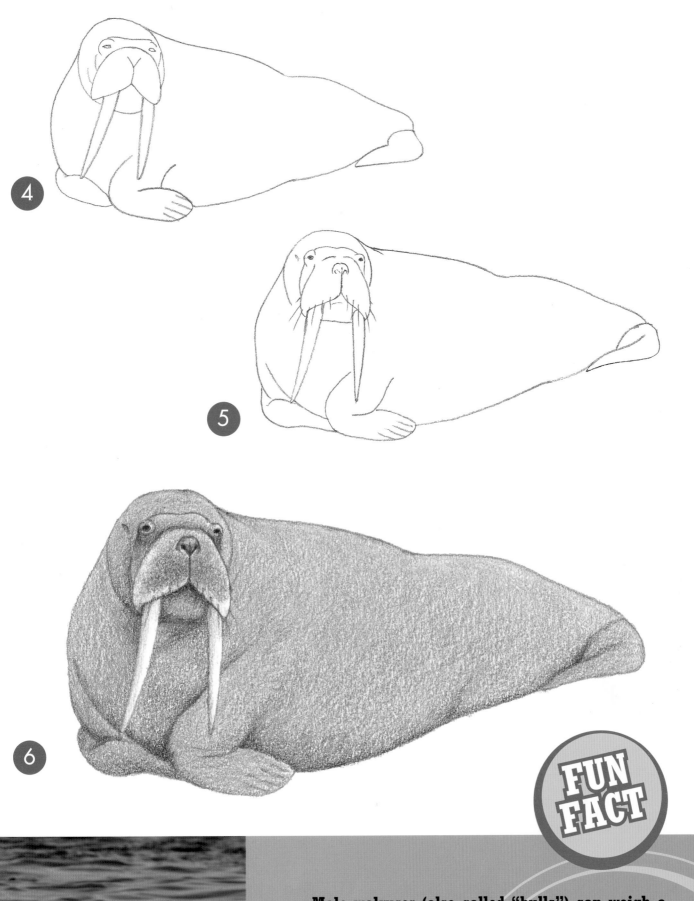

4

5

6

Male walruses (also called "bulls") can weigh a whopping 3,700 pounds! As a result, they have to use their strong tusks to help pull themselves out of the water and onto the ice. During mating season, the bulls also use their long tusks to protect their female "cows" from other male walruses.

Koala

This soft, **woolly** tree-dweller suspends its **short,** round body by clinging to eucalyptus trees—both its home and its food.

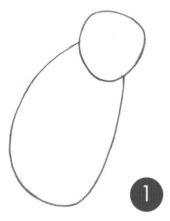

1

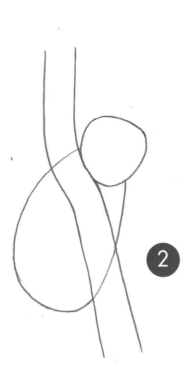

2

3

4

5

QUICK QUIZ!

Question: What do you call a baby koala?

The answer is at the bottom of the page.

6

Although eucalyptus leaves are the koala's primary source of food, this animal is a very picky eater. With over 600 eucalyptus varieties available, koalas eat only about 40 types and prefer just a select 10–12. As eucalyptus leaves don't provide much nutrition, koalas move slowly and sleep up to 20 hours a day to conserve energy.

FUN FACT

jellyfish

A jellyfish looks like a **bell** with **ribbons** trailing behind it. But don't be fooled by its beauty: the "ribbons" are *tentacles* that sting!

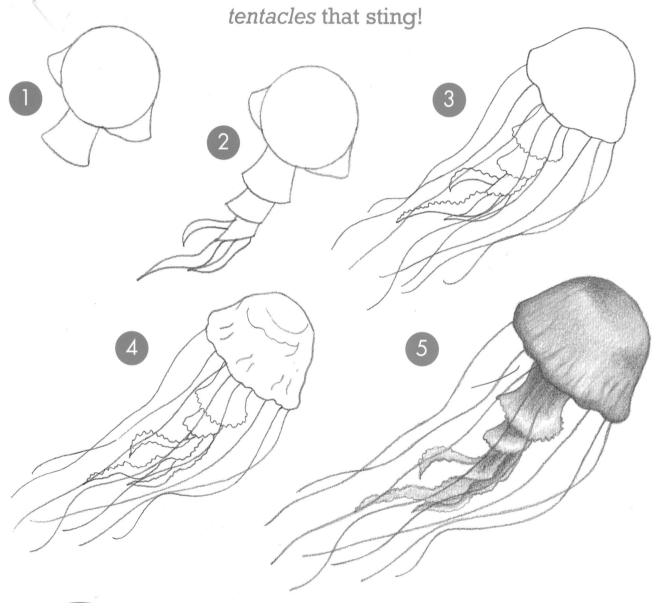

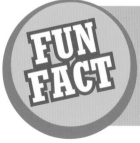

FUN FACT

Surprisingly the jellyfish has no lungs, gills, or any internal organs for breathing. Instead it "breathes" through the thin walls of its body and its long, stringy tentacles.

Hyena

The **spotted** hyena has many **doglike** features, but its large, rounded ears and sloping back give this animal a unique appearance.

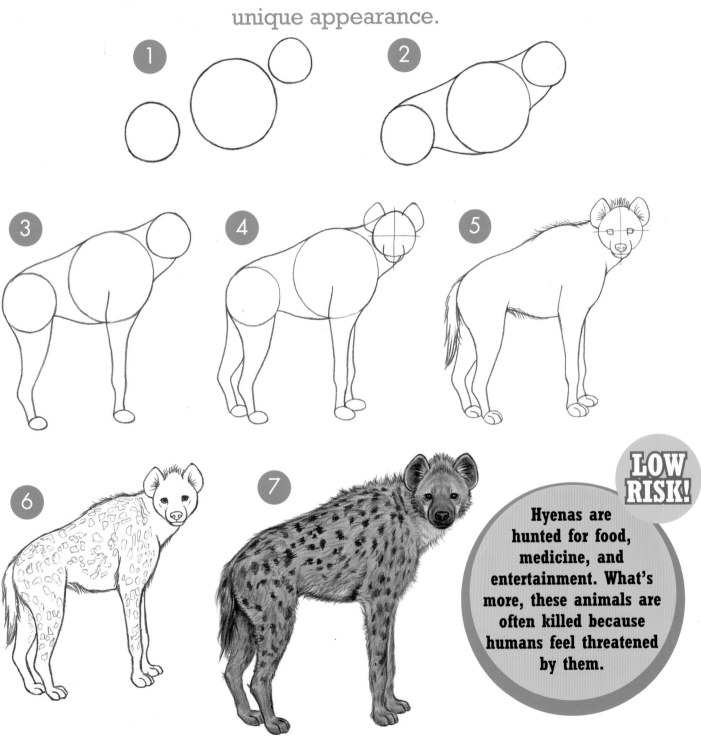

LOW RISK!

Hyenas are hunted for food, medicine, and entertainment. What's more, these animals are often killed because humans feel threatened by them.

Tiger Shark

Why is the tiger shark so **easy** to **pick out** in a lineup? Because it has dark markings on its back that resemble a tiger's stripes!

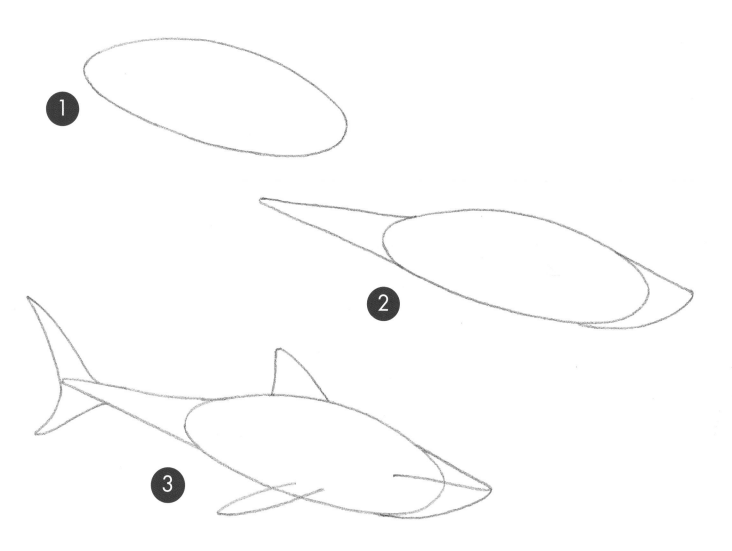

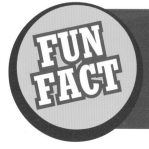

FUN FACT

Tiger sharks are known as the "wastebaskets of the sea" because they will eat just about anything, including people, old tires, and license plates!

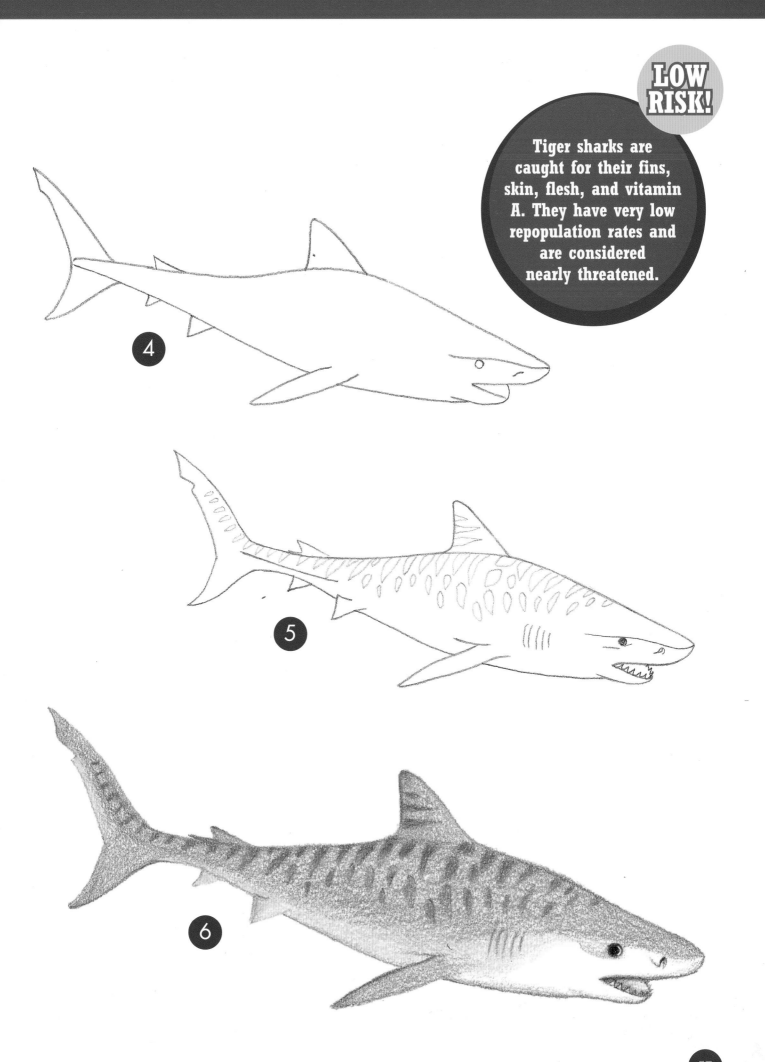

Tiger sharks are caught for their fins, skin, flesh, and vitamin A. They have very low repopulation rates and are considered nearly threatened.

4

5

6

Spider Monkey

Black-handed spider monkeys are **small** and **thin.** Their hands, feet, and heads are black, and black masks frame their round eyes.

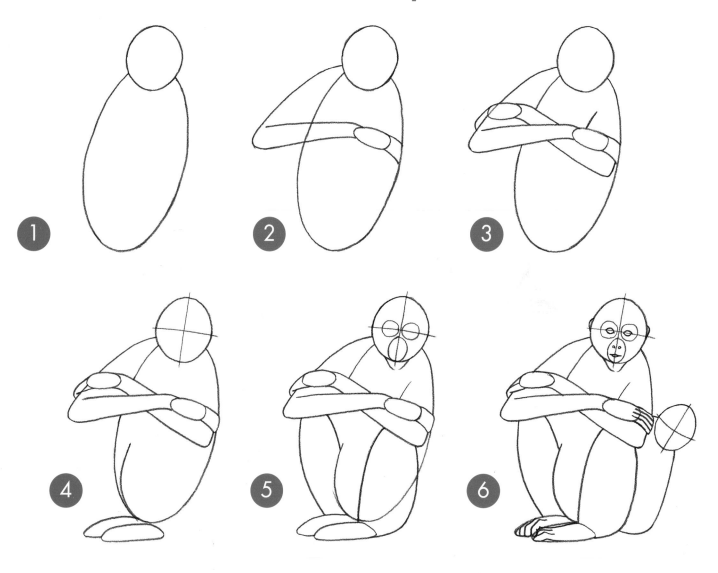

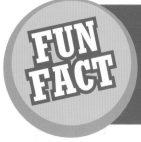

The black-handed spider monkey has a thriving population, even though about 70% of its Central American habitat has been lost.

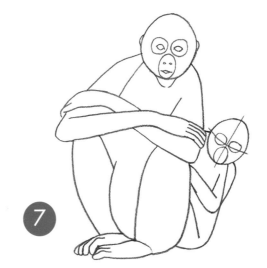

7

8

9

10

Swordfish

This fish's long, sharp **bill** resembles a **sword,** creating a streamlined shape that's perfect for speedy swimming!

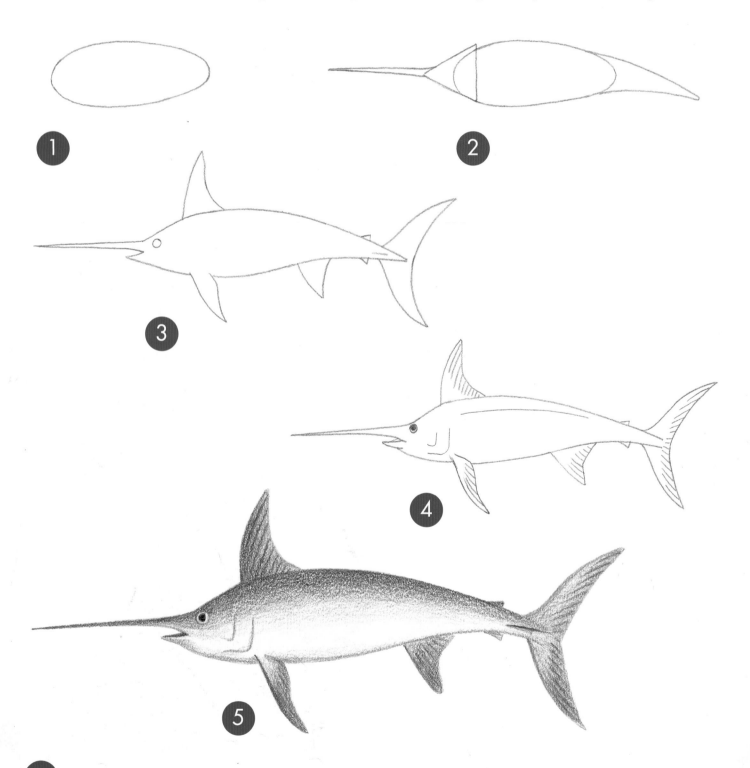

Orangutan

Every orangutan has a **bare** face, **round** eyes, and small ears, but only the male has large, round cheek pads and a long, hairy beard.

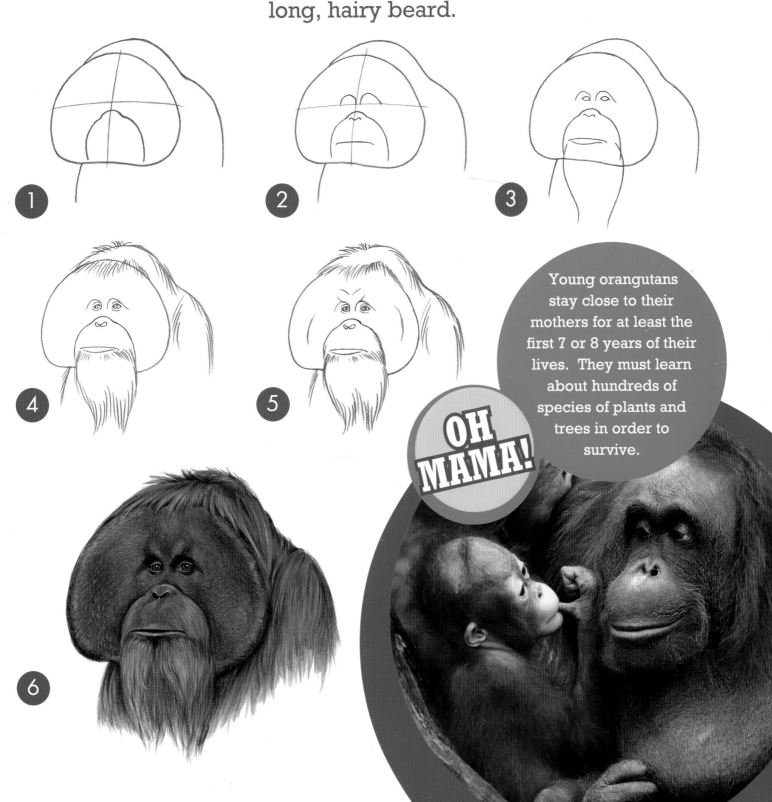

1

2

3

4

5

Young orangutans stay close to their mothers for at least the first 7 or 8 years of their lives. They must learn about hundreds of species of plants and trees in order to survive.

OH MAMA!

6

Sea Lion

Start this sea lion with a **circle** for the head and an **oval** for the body. Then finish with a velvety brown coat!

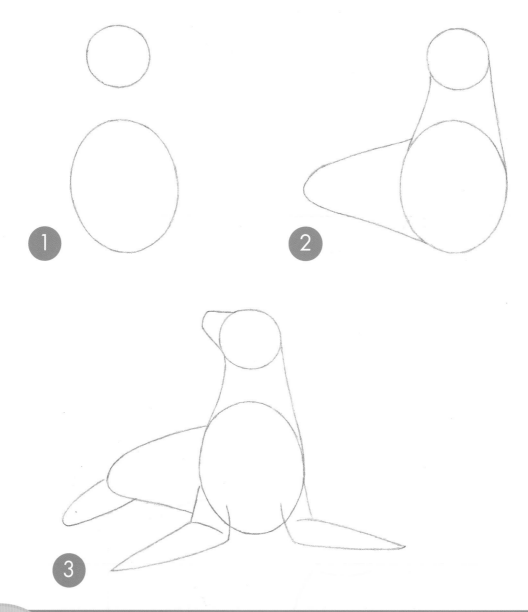

1

2

3

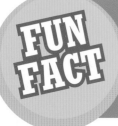

FUN FACT

When a sea lion swims, its front flippers push it forward while its back flippers steer. To help the sea lion move on land, the back flippers can also rotate forward under its body, acting as feet!

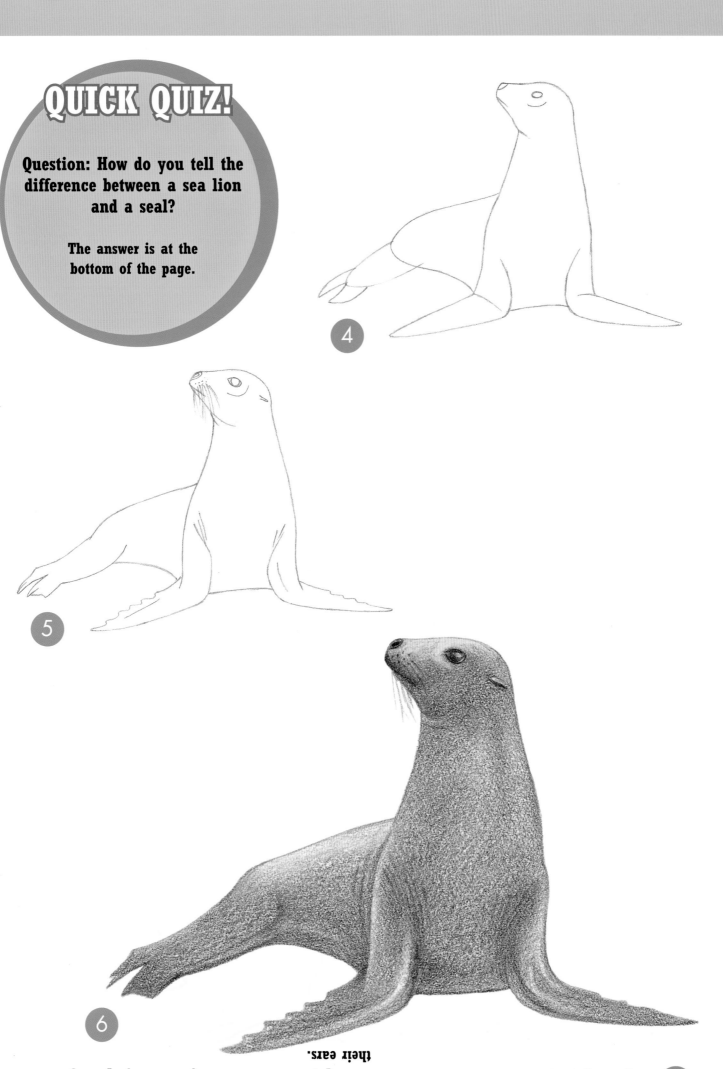

QUICK QUIZ!

Question: How do you tell the difference between a sea lion and a seal?

The answer is at the bottom of the page.

4

5

6

Rhinoceros

The **short** legs of this white rhino support its **bulky** body, and it uses its two curved, triangular-shaped horns to dig for food and defend itself!

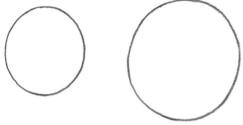

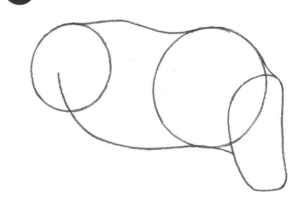

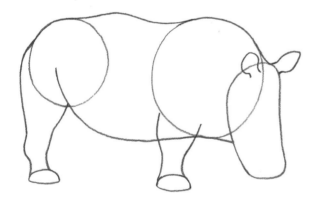

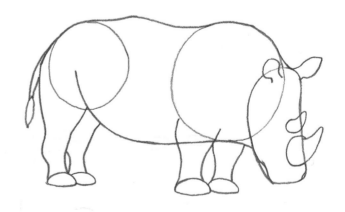

In Africa, the white rhino population suffers due to habitat loss. But illegal hunting (called "poaching") is also a threat to this rhino's survival.

HIGH RISK!

Orca

The **black** and **white** markings on an orca—or "killer whale"—make this amazing animal easy to identify!

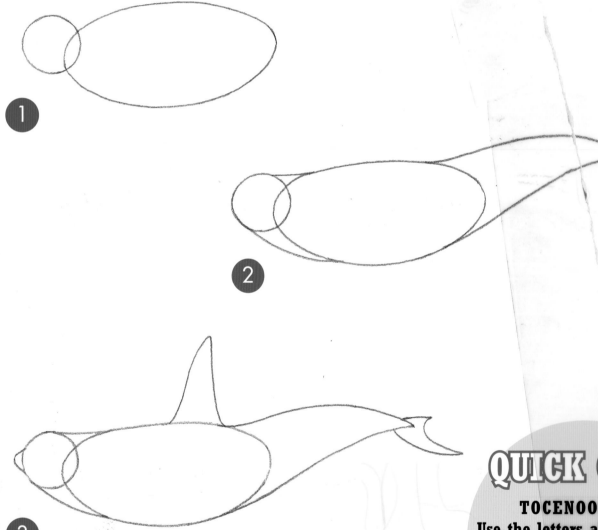

1

2

3

4

5

6

The orca is an extremely skilled hunter, giving it the nickname "killer whale." But although it feeds on a wide range of prey—from small fish to blue whales—a wild orca has never been known to kill a human.

Tapir

What's **black** and **white** with a long curved snout? The Malayan tapir! This "living fossil" has looked exactly the same for 30 million years!

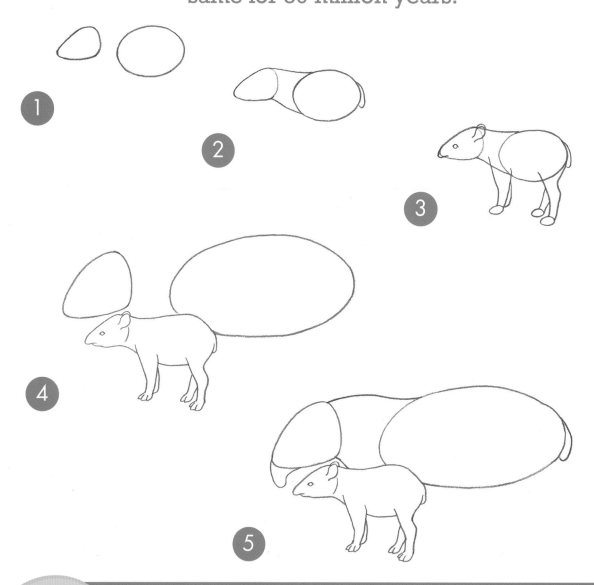

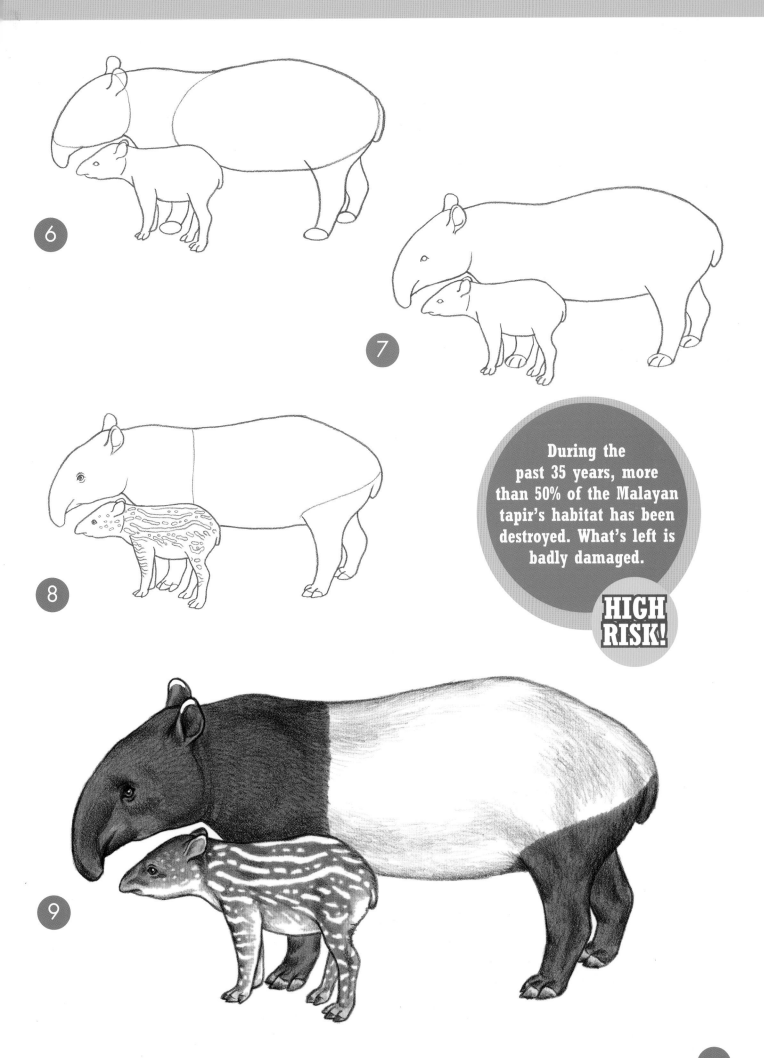

6

7

8

During the past 35 years, more than 50% of the Malayan tapir's habitat has been destroyed. What's left is badly damaged.

HIGH RISK!

9

Hammerhead

This shark is named for its **flat, T-shaped** head, and its eyes and nostrils are located on opposite sides.

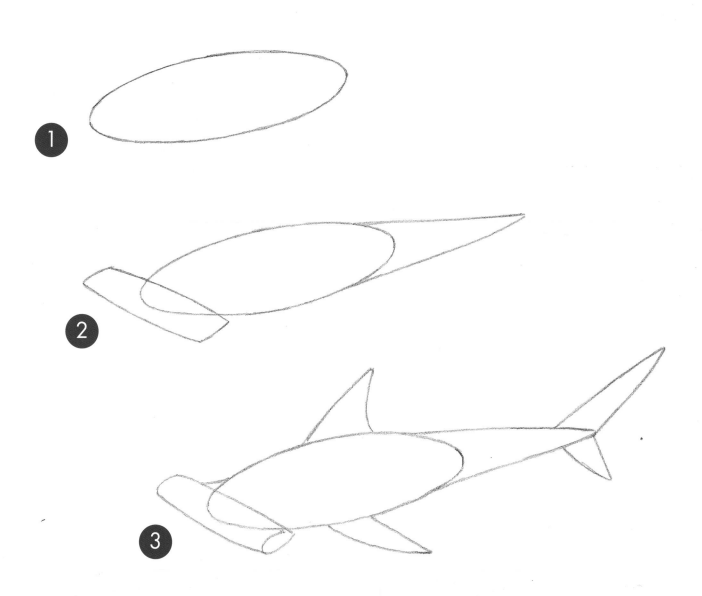

1

2

3

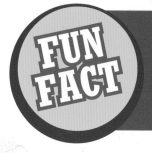

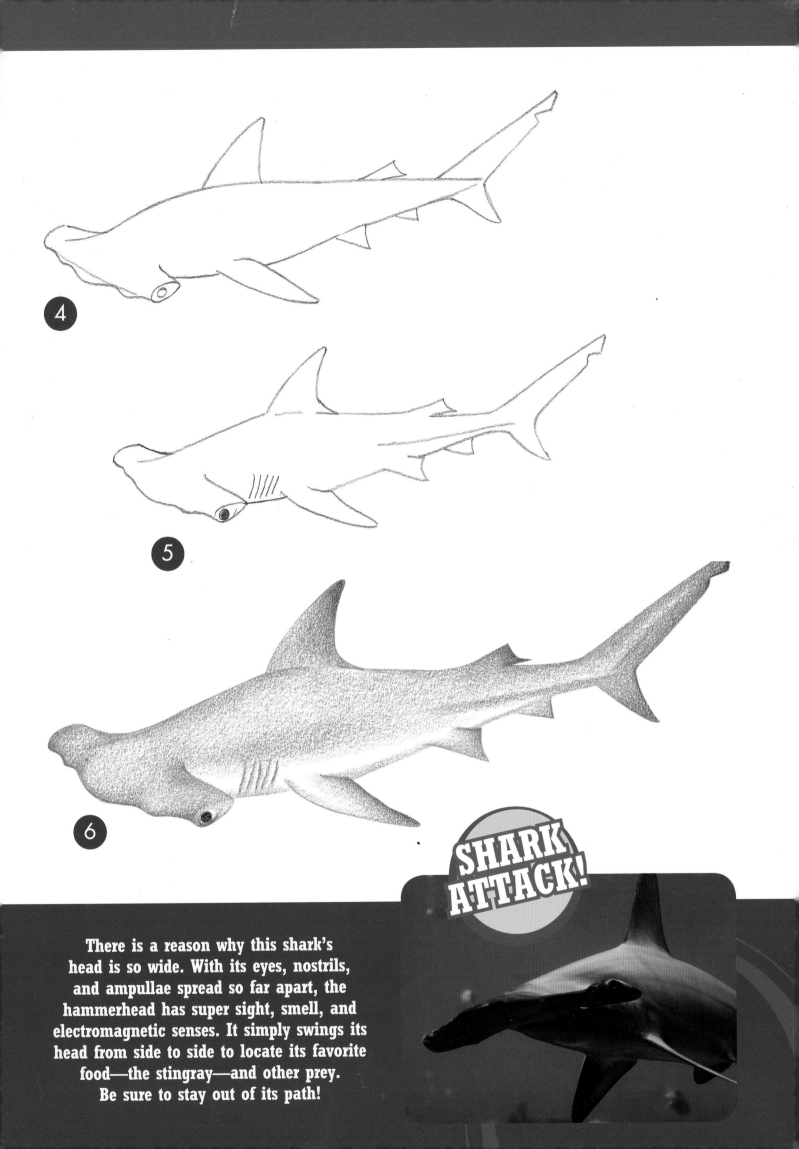

4

5

6

There is a reason why this shark's head is so wide. With its eyes, nostrils, and ampullae spread so far apart, the hammerhead has super sight, smell, and electromagnetic senses. It simply swings its head from side to side to locate its favorite food—the stingray—and other prey. Be sure to stay out of its path!

Okapi

Its **stripes** make the okapi look like a zebra, but this **tall,** two-toned animal has the long legs and flexible neck of a giraffe.

AT RISK!
The okapi is quickly losing its habitat to human farms, roads, and homes. And this animal is also hunted as a source of food.

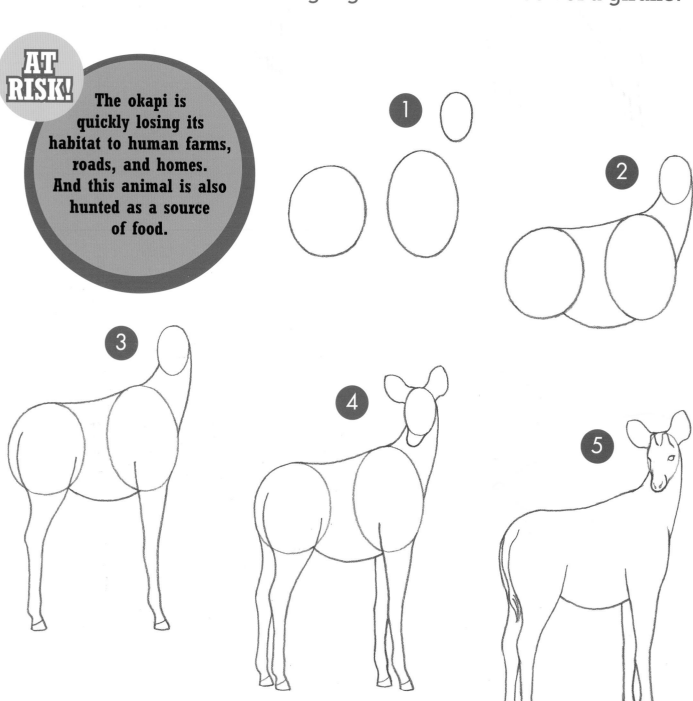

6

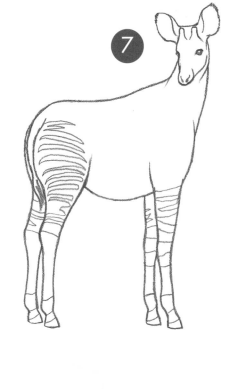

7

8

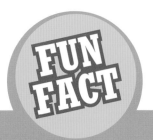

FUN FACT

The okapi lives only in the tropical forests of north-eastern Zaire, on the African continent, where it hides itself in the thick vegetation. A very shy animal, the okapi is rarely seen in the wild. Because of this, the okapi was thought to be a "forest zebra" until 1900, when it was finally recognized as its own unique species of animal. The okapi has no relation to the zebra, but it is the only known relative of the giraffe.

Octopus

The octopus has a **soft,** oval body and **eight** arms covered with bubblelike suction cups.

Quick Quiz Answer: True! An octopus can mimic the colors and patterns of its surroundings.

74

4

5

QUICK QUIZ!

TRUE or FALSE?
An octopus can hide
in plain sight of
dangerous predators.

The answer is at the bottom
of the opposite page.

FUN FACT

This animal doesn't just have multiple arms—it has multiple hearts too! An octopus has three hearts: two for pumping blood through its gills to get oxygen, and one for pumping blood through its entire body.

Zebra

From its **black** muzzle to the tips of its **long** ears, the zebra's face is covered in narrow stripes; its body and mane have broader stripes.

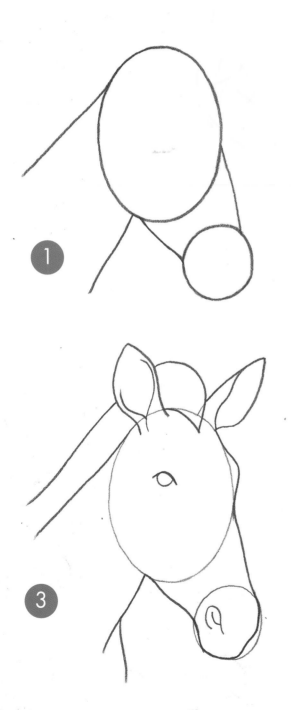

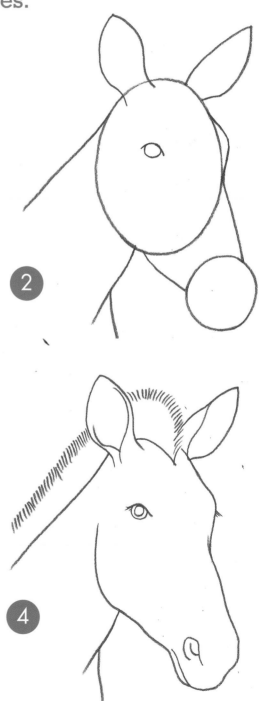

5

6

FUN
FACT

Experts aren't exactly sure why zebras
have stripes, but they think that the
markings serve some sort of purpose.
The stripes might help the animals
recognize other members of their
herd, regulate temperature, or
confuse predators.

Seahorse

This **critter** has a **horselike** head; a spiky, S-shaped body; and a long, curled tail.

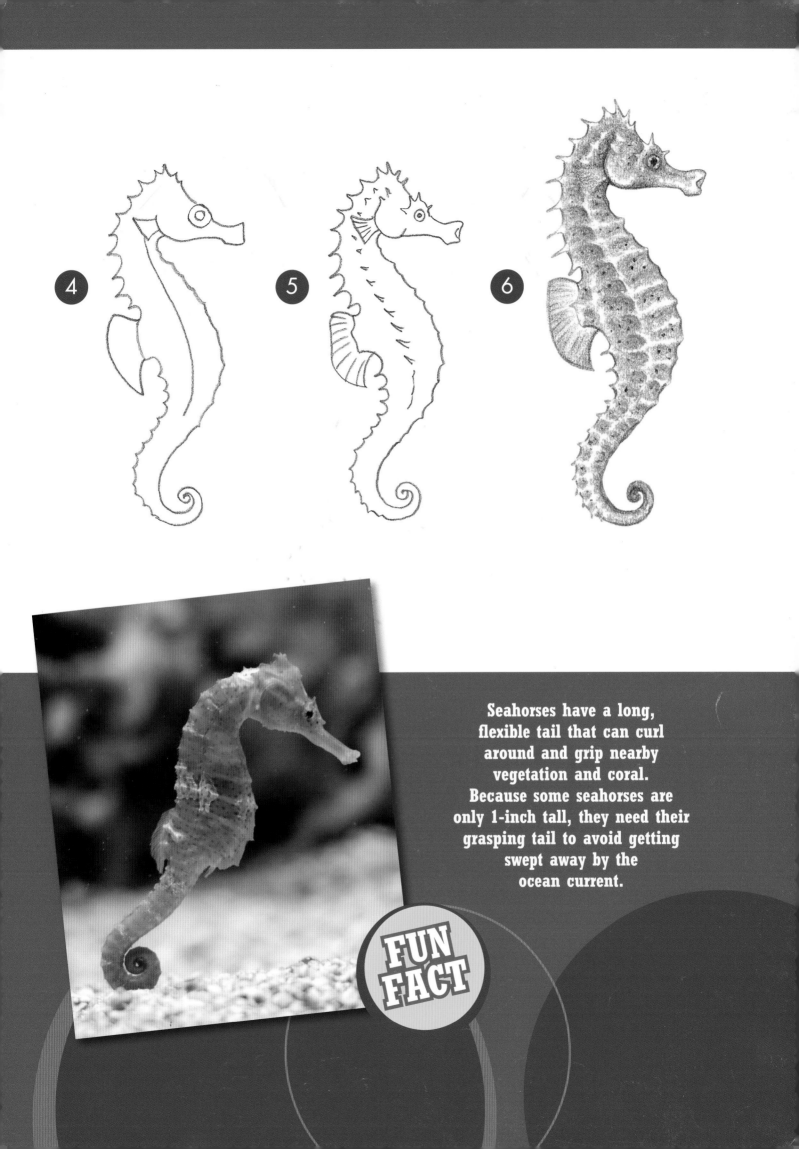

Seahorses have a long, flexible tail that can curl around and grip nearby vegetation and coral. Because some seahorses are only 1-inch tall, they need their grasping tail to avoid getting swept away by the ocean current.

FUN FACT

Glossary

Amphibious (AM-fib-ee-iss) - To be able to live on land and in water.

Ampullae (AM-pew-lay) - Special organs on sharks that can detect electrical fields around prey.

Camouflage (CAM-o-flaj) - To hide by blending in with the surroundings.

Cartilage (CAR-ti-lij) - A tough, flexible tissue that is softer than bone and found in sharks.

Crustacean (crus-TAY-shin) - An animal that usually lives in water and has a hard outer shell and several pairs of legs.

Echolocation (E-ko-lo-cay-shin) - How dolphins and whales locate objects by sending out sounds and studying their echoes.

Exoskeleton (EK-so-ske-le-tin) - A hard, outer covering, such as the shell of a turtle or lobster.

Extinct (EK-stinct) - No longer living or existing.

Habitat (HAB-i-tat) - Where an animal lives, such as the ocean or desert.

Mammal (MA-mol) - A warm-blooded animal that has hair, gives birth to live young, and feeds its young milk, such as a human or bear.

Predator (PRE-da-tur) - An animal that kills and eats other animals.

Tentacle (TEN-ta-kul) - A long, flexible organ that grows near the mouth of an animal, such as a jellyfish or octopus, used for feeding or grasping.

Salsa Cooking

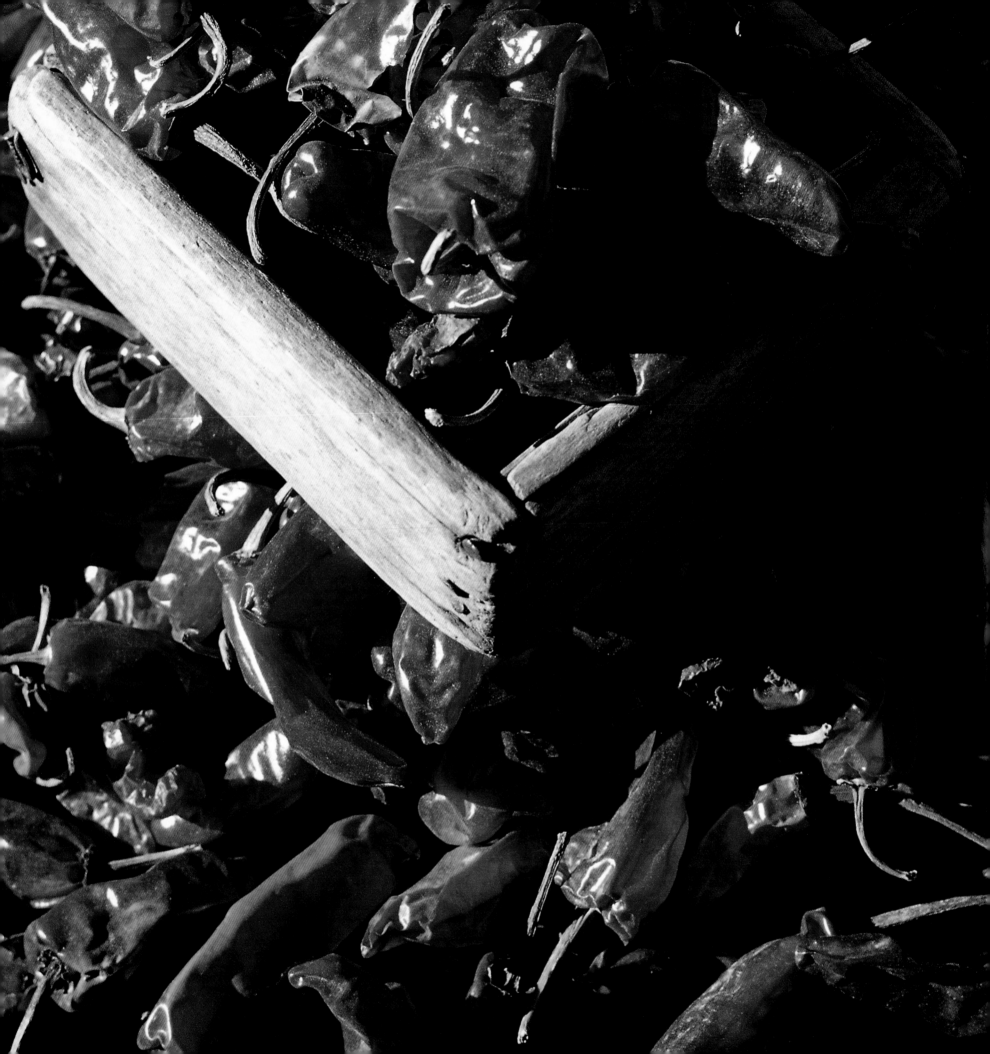

SALSA COOKING

Marjie Lambert

NEW
BURLINGTON
BOOKS

DEDICATION

To my brothers, Ken and Robert, captive
audience to my earliest cooking experiments, and
my sisters-in-law, Nicky and Laveda, who now
have to put up with their eccentric tastes.

A QUINTET BOOK

Published by New Burlington Books
6 Blundell Street
London N7 9BH

ISBN 1-85348-652-3

This book was designed and produced by
Quintet Publishing Limited
6 Blundell Street
London N7 9BH

Creative Director: Richard Dewing
Designer: Kerry Quested @ Design Revolution,
Brighton
Project Editor: Helen Denholm
Editor: Jane Middleton
Food Photographer: Andrew Sydenham
Home Economy: Nicola Fowler and Deborah
Greatrex

PICTURE CREDITS

Russell and Pamela Bamert: pages 11, 13, 25, 32,
39, 56, 110.
Travel Ink Photo & Feature Library: pages 45, 50.
Trip (© Richard Powers): page 29.
Peter Wilson: pages 2, 68, 81, 90, 96, 128.

ACKNOWLEDGEMENTS

With thanks to my friends George and Karen, to
Helen at Quintet, and as always to Terry.

Typeset in Great Britain by
Central Southern Typesetters, Eastbourne
Manufactured in Singapore by Eray Scan Pte Ltd
Printed in Singapore by Star Standard Pte Ltd

contents

INTRODUCTION

Most people think of salsa as a spicy tomato-onion-chile sauce to eat with chips or tacos. However, there's much more to it than that. As the popularity of salsa has increased, it has come to mean sauces, relishes, and even chopped salads that almost always include some type of chile but may not include tomatoes or onions. Instead, the main ingredient may be fruit, black beans, corn, or even unexpected vegetables like radishes or zucchini.

The definition of salsa has to be elastic. As soon as you find a rule, you find the exception. Not every salsa contains chiles. Typically salsa is used as a condiment, but some, such as Black Bean-Corn Salsa, are so hearty that they need no accompaniment. Salsas may be raw or cooked, but often in an uncooked salsa some of the ingredients are broiled or roasted to add flavor or mellow a raw taste.

Salsas go with all kinds of food. In addition to chips, they are marvelous with broiled meats and seafood, on eggs, over pasta, in salad, stirred into steamed vegetables and, of course, over Mexican dishes like tacos and chiles rellenos. Some salsas are even served with ice cream.

The word salsa is Spanish for sauce, and salsas have their roots in Mexico. However, they have long been a fixture in the Caribbean, South and Central America, and the southwestern United States, too. In the 1990s, the passion for salsa has spread into other parts of the United States and Europe. In 1992, North Americans spent twice as much on salsas and other Mexican sauces as they did on ketchup, formerly their favorite condiment, and sales of salsa are still growing.

More than 2,000 brands of salsa are available in the United States. Increasingly, they are not the bottled varieties that have been stocked for years in the foreign-food sections of grocery stores, but are fresh, uncooked salsas sitting in the refrigerated deli or produce sections. In the bottling process, salsas are heated to nearly 200°F, eliminating their fresh taste and much of their texture. While bottled salsas still dominate the market, a growing share is being taken over by specialty and gourmet salsas at the expense of the big brands that have been around for years – evidence that people are looking for more adventurous tastes in their salsas. Salsa ingredients, especially a growing range of fresh and dried chiles, are also gaining shelf space.

It is not difficult to see why salsa has become so popular. North Americans are fascinated by ethnic foods, particularly spicy ones, and the cuisine of the United States has become a culinary melting pot. Convenience is a priority, and most salsas are easy to make. Salsa meets the current demand for healthful foods. Made of fresh fruit or vegetables, chiles, herbs, and just a dash of olive oil, salsa is often a healthful alternative to traditional sauces heavy with fat and cream. And it tastes good.

Paul Prudhomme, the gregarious promoter of Cajun food, likes to talk about food creating a "round" sensation in the mouth, with different flavors setting off different tastebuds, until the whole palate is dancing. A good, fresh salsa has much the same effect. It is a marvelous mix of flavors, some subtle, some aggressive, accompanied by the kick of hot chiles.

In this book, you will find more than 40 salsa recipes. They range from variations on the basic tomato-onion-chile mix, to black bean salsas, corn salsas, fruit salsas, and salsas based on roasted chiles. There are raw salsas and cooked salsas; winter salsas, for when tomatoes and chiles are out of season, and even dessert salsas for spooning over ice cream. Hopefully, you will find inspiration for your own creations, using these recipes as a basis.

There are also plenty of ideas on how to use the salsas, with recipes for appetizers, soups, salads, side dishes, main courses and desserts. While the list of salsa recipes is meant to be comprehensive, the range of other recipes in this book is not. Instead, they are intended to be a sampling of what is possible, a starting point for your own imagination.

INGREDIENTS

CHILES

Chiles are grown all around the world – consider the sweet pimento that produces Hungary's famous paprika, the hot red Thai chile, and the incendiary Scotch bonnet of the Caribbean. However, Mexico is king when it comes to chiles, with about 100 varieties, only a few of which are commonly available outside Mexico.

Buying chiles can be a very frustrating experience because they are frequently mislabeled or not labeled at all. Many grocery stores stock several varieties of fresh chiles and tell you only what you can see for yourself, that they are red or green. You are left to guess whether they are Anaheims or serranos, habaneros or poblanos, and even how hot they are. Dried chiles are often mislabeled by the packager, in part because the same chile will have different names in different parts of Mexico. It is a good idea to learn to identify your favorite varieties on sight.

All chiles belong to the *Capsicum* family. Their heat comes from capsaicin, a compound that is concentrated not in the seeds, as is commonly believed, but in the white fleshy placenta and veins, particularly around the stem. Cut open a jalapeño chile and you will probably see thin streaks of orange running through the veins – that is capsaicin. You can adjust the level of heat in a recipe by removing all the veins and seeds for a milder dish or leaving them for a hotter dish.

In 1902 Wilbur Scoville, a pharmacologist, searched for a way to rank the relative heat of chiles. He mixed ground chiles with sugar, alcohol and water, then graded them according to how much the substance had to be diluted before no heat was detectable. Now the same ranking is done by computerized technology; zero for bell peppers, 10,000 for jalapeños, 35,000 for serranos, and 150,000 to 200,000 for habaneros and Scotch bonnet chiles.

FRESH CHILES

The chiles below are listed according to their strength, from the mildest to the hottest. However, it is difficult to give an exact guide, since the same type of chile can vary widely in heat, depending on the growing conditions.

Anaheim Also known as the California chile, this is pale green, 5 to 7 inches long, skinny, and relatively flat. Mild in flavor, it is good roasted and peeled, and is often stuffed and used in chiles rellenos.

New Mexico The New Mexico chile resembles the Anaheim, although it is a little hotter. Green New Mexico chiles are available for only a short time each fall outside New Mexico. Most are allowed to ripen to a bright red and are then dried. They are available in their dried form, and are the type used in *ristras,* hanging bunches of dried chiles.

Poblano These green-black chiles have broad shoulders, narrowing to the tip, and resemble dark, emaciated bell peppers. Moderately spicy, they are never eaten raw, but are roasted and peeled. They are often used in chiles rellenos. Poblanos are often incorrectly called pasillas, both in their fresh and dried state.

7

SUBSTITUTING CHILES

Although markets carry more varieties of chiles than they did just a few years ago, it isn't always possible to find a particular chile specified in a recipe. Feel free to substitute one chile for another, keeping in mind any difference in their heat. Remember that the salsa's heat is affected as much by how closely you trim the seeds and veins as by the type of chile you use.

Some tips for substituting chiles:

▶ Bell peppers contain none of the substance that causes chiles to be hot, and should not be used as a substitute for chiles.

▶ Unless you're trying to increase or decrease the spiciness of the salsa, try to find another chile that has approximately the same degree of heat as the one called for in the recipe. While a serrano chile is an excellent substitute for a jalapeño, an Anaheim is not. No matter how many Anaheims you put in the salsa, it will not be as hot as a jalapeño salsa.

▶ Some of the larger chiles with tougher skins, such as poblanos and Anaheims, are usually roasted and peeled before they are added to salsa. Although substituting roast chiles for raw – or vice versa – will change the character of the salsa, the flavor will still be good.

▶ If all you can find are dried chiles, choose a cooked salsa recipe. It is difficult to make a good uncooked salsa with reconstituted dried chiles.

Jalapeño These glossy green chiles are probably the most widely used variety outside Mexico. They are smooth-skinned, narrow, and about 3 inches long. Although they are hot, their heat is much reduced if they are seeded and veined. They can be used raw, roasted, pickled, smoked, or dried. If left to ripen, they turn red.

8

Serrano Slightly hotter than jalapeños, these are small, about 2 inches long and very skinny. They are ripe when dark green, but if left on the plant will continue ripening to a bright red. They are most often eaten raw in salsas.

Habanero These chiles of the Yucatan, along with the related Scotch bonnet of the Caribbean, are just about the hottest chiles in creation. The habanero is only occasionally

available in the United States but is commonly used as an ingredient in bottled hot sauces. It looks like a miniature bell pepper or lantern, perhaps 2 inches long, and its color can range from green to orange-red.

Other fresh chiles occasionally available in the United States are the **cayenne,** long, skinny, bright red and hot, most commonly dried and ground into cayenne pepper; the **cubanelle,** a long and skinny yellow or pale green chile, most often seen on the East Coast – mild and sweet, it can be substituted for Anaheim chiles; the **pasilla,** also known as chile negro, a slim purple-black chile that is moderately spicy, like the poblano; the **fresno,** sometimes called wax chile or chile caribe, a very hot chile that is similar in size to the jalapeño but a bit more triangular, and ranges from pale green to bright red. Fresno chiles are also sometimes called **chile gueros,** which is actually a generic name for pale green or yellow chiles.

DRIED CHILES
California These are dried Anaheims, mild, long, skinny and red-brown.

Ancho This is the dried version of the poblano. It has a very pleasant spiciness that is hot but still easily tolerable. The ancho is often mislabeled pasilla, but is distinguishable when held up to the light by its red-brown color; in the same light, a true pasilla is brown-black.

New Mexico The New Mexico chile, cousin to the Anaheim, is allowed to ripen until it is red and hot. It is widely available in dried form.

Cascabel Cascabel refers to both the fresh and dried form of this round, dark red-brown chile, but it is most often available dried. Medium hot and slightly fruity, it is good lightly toasted, then crumbled and added to sauces.

Chipotle This is the jalapeño chile, smoked and dried. It is hot, and adds a wonderful, smoky flavor to salsas and cooked dishes. It is also available canned in adobo sauce or pickled. Once you become familiar with the chipotle, you'll want to add it to everything!

Chile de Arbol This short, skinny, red-orange chile is very hot. It is usually a dried red serrano, but may also be one of the other small hot peppers such as cayenne or Thai. Unhelpful packagers may even label chile de Arbol simply as "red chiles."

MISCELLANEOUS

Chile flakes, or dried crushed chiles Sometimes sold as chiles caribe, these are usually dried, crushed New Mexico red chiles, and are hot. They are the chile flakes often seen in pizza parlors.

Chili powder Chili powder is a commercial seasoning mix that includes ground chiles and other spices. It is only mildly to moderately spicy. Pure ground dried chile powder is more typically available in the Mexican section than the spice section of the grocery store. It is usually hotter than chili powder, but how hot depends on the type of chile. Most common are California chile powder, consisting of dried ground Anaheims, and a hotter powder usually made with chimayo chiles from New Mexico. Cayenne and paprika are also dried, ground chiles.

Canned chiles Except for chipotle chiles, canned chiles are not recommended, since they lose much of their taste and texture in processing.

TOMATOES

If chiles are the diva of salsa, tomatoes are the chorus. When they're good, they provide a solid – and often unnoticed – background for the star. But when they're bad, they mar the entire performance. Try to avoid grocery-store tomatoes, the hard, pink, flavorless kind. Some stores now stock "vine-ripened" (as opposed to chemically ripened) tomatoes, usually at a higher price. Buy the riper ones. Alternatively, buy Romas, small Italian tomatoes that are meatier and travel better than larger tomatoes, so they may be riper. You can also use canned whole tomatoes, or broil the hard tomatoes, a process that adds flavor even to the worst grocery-store tomatoes. Best of all, grow your own or buy just-picked tomatoes from a farmer's market.

ONIONS

Onions are a crucial ingredient in most salsas. They are good both raw and roasted. Use white or yellow onions unless the recipe specifies otherwise. Red onions are also excellent in salsas, although the flat Spanish reds do not hold up well in cooking. Green onions, or scallions, add a sharp flavor and a crunch to uncooked salsas. Sweet onions, such as Vidalias or Maui sweets, are becoming more widely available and can add a different twist to salsas.

TOMATILLOS

Because of their appearance, tomatillos are sometimes called green tomatoes, or little tomatoes, and they are often used in place of tomatoes in salsa. In fact they are members of the gooseberry family. They have a papery outer husk that must be removed, and they should be rinsed to get rid of the sticky residue on the surface of the husked tomatillo. Peek under the husk to see how ripe they are. Bright green tomatillos are not ripe; look for pale green to yellowish ones. If you use unripe tomatillos, the salsa will be tart. You can add a little sugar to offset the tartness.

GARLIC

Garlic is a staple in many salsas. Use fresh minced garlic, never garlic powder or salt. Bottled minced garlic is acceptable. Roasting or baking garlic mellows its sharp taste and gives salsas a good flavor.

AVOCADOS

There are two commonly available types of avocados. The most flavorful is the Haas, which has black, bumpy skin and is plentiful in late spring through early fall. The Fuerte has a greener, smoother skin and is not as flavorful, but is available during the winter. Avocados can be temperamental, seemingly going from hard and flavorless to mushy and bad-tasting in little more than a day. The best way to use avocados is to buy them a few days in advance of when you want to use them, while they are still hard, then let them ripen on your kitchen counter, away from direct sunlight. They will ripen slightly faster if you close them in a paper bag with an apple. Do not refrigerate them before they are ripe. Once they are ripe, they will hold for a day or two in the refrigerator. In an emergency, add a little avocado oil to improve the flavor of a mashed, not-quite-ripe avocado.

9

BELL PEPPERS AND SWEET CHILES

Although they are related to chiles, bell peppers do not contain any capsaicin and cannot be substituted for chiles. Green bell peppers are only occasionally added to salsa. The sweet red pepper – which is simply a ripe green bell pepper – is more frequently used, either raw or roasted. Because of its sweetness, the raw red pepper marries well with fruit salsas and adds crunch. Roasted and peeled, it is a delicious savory addition to many salsas. Other sweet or mild chiles, such as the Italian sweet chile or the Hungarian pimento, can be added to salsa for texture and flavor, although they are not a substitute for spicy chiles. Remove veins and seeds before using.

10

FRUITS

Fruit salsas are more popular in the Caribbean and the United States than in Mexico. They are excellent with broiled meats and seafood. Tropical fruits, especially mango, papaya and pineapple, are surprisingly good when combined with hot chiles, and are often broiled for a sweet smoky flavor. Broiled pineapple is particularly good. **Mangoes** should be firm but not hard – slightly less ripe for salsas than for eating plain – and yellow to red-orange (although some new varieties of mango are ripe when green). If not picked too green, they can be ripened on the kitchen counter. **Papayas** should be yellow with no more than a few green streaks, and no soft spots; they will ripen a little at home. **Pineapple** should be more gold than green, with no soft spots, and should have a sweet

perfume. They do not ripen after they are picked. **Peaches** and **nectarines** should be slightly soft. They will ripen on the counter or in a paper bag if they were not picked too green.

JICAMA

This Mexican tuber with crisp white flesh and a thin brown skin should be peeled and eaten raw. It has a very mild flavor and is valued mostly for the crunch it adds to salsas and salads. In Mexico, slices of raw jicama are drizzled with lime juice and sprinkled with chili powder, then eaten as a snack.

BEANS

Beans are a staple of the Latin American diet, so it is not surprising that they are a popular ingredient in, or partner to, salsa. Black beans, also known as turtle beans, are the usual type in salsas. They have a smoky, nutty flavor, but need salt and other herbs or spices to complement it.

CHORIZO

Chorizo is a spicy Mexican sausage, most often made with pork but sometimes with beef. Paprika is usually the predominant spice, but the ingredients may vary widely, and the seasonings in a dish containing chorizo should

be adjusted accordingly. The fat content also varies. Chorizo adds excellent flavor to beans and eggs.

HERBS AND SPICES

CILANTRO

The most popular herb or spice used in salsa is cilantro, a pungent member of the parsley family. Also known as coriander or Chinese parsley, fresh cilantro is available in most grocery stores. Dried cilantro is almost never used in salsa, and coriander seeds are not a substitute for fresh cilantro. Look for cilantro with bright green leaves, and with roots attached. Pick off yellow leaves and store in a plastic bag in the refrigerator, with roots, but not the leaves, wrapped in a wet paper towel.

CUMIN

Cumin seed, native to the Mediterranean, is a staple in Mexican cooking. In the United States it is more frequently used in its ground form, although some cooks like to toast and grind the seeds themselves. It is excellent with beans, and is occasionally used in salsas. Use it sparingly.

OREGANO

Choose Mexican oregano, which has a stronger flavor than the Greek, and use it in dried-leaf form, not ground. Some cooks like to toast oregano briefly in an ungreased skillet before using. Be careful not to scorch it.

Other herbs occasionally used in salsa are **basil,** which marries well with tomatoes although it is not a traditional salsa ingredient; fresh **mint,** which also goes well with tomatoes, and with some fruit salsas; fresh **ginger,** seen more often in Caribbean salsas; and **epazote,** a medicinally flavored weed also known as wormseed or Mexican tea, which is hard to find in the United States, but is popular in southern Mexico in salsas and bean dishes.

COOKING TECHNIQUES

Once making salsa was easy: you simply chopped tomatoes, onions, chiles, and perhaps some cilantro or another herb, added a squeeze of lime juice and a pinch of salt, and you had salsa. But now that salsa has become so popular, there are all sorts of variations on the basic theme, such as roasting ingredients to give a good, rich flavor, or cooking salsa for a more concentrated sauce. Food processors have made a difference too, and if they are not used with care they can turn what should be a rough-textured mix of distinct ingredients into a mushy soup. The chunky textures are part of a salsa's charm. Below are some pointers for successful salsa making.

Strings of chiles for sale at the Hatch Chile Festival in New Mexico.

PROTECTING YOUR SKIN

The capsaicin in chiles can burn your skin, and what's worse, if you get it on your hands you're likely to get it in your eyes, too. You don't realize how often you rub your eyes and touch the tender skin on your face until you do it with capsaicin on your hands. It's particularly painful if you get it in your contact lenses. Never touch your lenses if you have been handling chiles; your eyes are far more sensitive than your hands, and a little tingle on your fingertip will turn into sharp pain in your eye. The solution is to wear rubber gloves when working with chiles. Even a plastic sandwich bag will do. In moments of desperation, use a piece of plastic wrap to protect your hand.

If you do get capsaicin on your hands, running plain water over them won't help, since capsaicin is not water-soluble. At worst, water will spread the pain. Soap up the spot, then rinse. Sometimes it helps to massage shortening into the skin, then wash it off with soap and water.

ROASTING AND GRILLING

Roasting adds flavor to salsa ingredients. Even hard, insipid grocery-store tomatoes are improved by roasting over an open flame. The process also blisters chile and pepper skins and makes them easy to remove. Another advantage of roasting is that it cooks out much of the excess juice from tomatoes, so that you don't end up with a pool of watery tomato juice in your salsa.

Traditional Mexican roasting involves using a comal, or Mexican griddle. Cast-iron skillets are, however, an acceptable substitute. Grilling over an open flame is the preferred method, but roasting under a broiler is also effective, although of course it doesn't add the delicious smoky flavor.

Chiles and peppers can be roasted whole or cut into large, flat sections. Turn the skin side toward the heat source, and check them frequently. The skin will blister slightly and develop some brown spots, and gradually become charred and completely blistered. Chiles with uneven surfaces, like poblanos, will not cook as evenly as a straight-sided red bell pepper, but that's okay. Be careful that the heat chars only the skin, not the flesh, and do not turn the fleshy side toward the heat. If you are roasting whole chiles, turn until all sides are done.

Remove the chiles or peppers from the heat when the skin is completely blistered and mostly browned or blackened. This can take just 2 or 3 minutes a side over flaming coals, or 10 minutes or longer under a broiler. Put the chiles or peppers in a plastic bag or a covered bowl and let them steam for about 10 minutes, then scrape or pull off the skin. It should come away easily, but it's okay if some bits of blackened skin remain; they will add to the flavor. Remember that cooking does not neutralize the capsaicin, so you still need to protect your skin. If you cooked the chiles or peppers whole, remove the seeds.

If you only need to roast one or two chiles, you can do so over the flame of a gas stove burner. Pinch the chile in long tongs or impale it on the end of a long fork, and hold it at the top of the flame. This process is as effective as the others, but it is time consuming since you can do only one at a time.

Dried chiles gain a tasty flavor from roasting. Put them in a 250°F oven for 5 minutes or so, or in an ungreased skillet, until they darken slightly and turn brittle. Do not allow them to blacken or they will taste bitter. Once roasted, they will crumble easily.

Roasting adds flavor to ***tomatoes,*** too, especially if it is done over an open flame. Cut the tomatoes in half horizontally and squeeze out most of the seeds and excess juice. Place with the skin side toward the heat, and cook

1. Roast or broil the chiles or peppers until the skin is mostly blackened.

2. Remove from the heat and place in a plastic bag or a covered bowl for about 10 minutes.

3. Scrape or pull off the skin. You can leave a few of the blackened bits for extra flavor.

until the skin is partly blackened and slips off easily. If you're cooking over an open flame, turn the cut side toward the flame and cook briefly. To cook tomatoes under a broiler, place them cut-side down on a broiler-safe baking sheet. If the baking sheet does not have edges, line it with foil and crimp the foil to create a shallow basin to catch the juice. When the tomatoes are done, slip off their skins and let the tomatoes cool in a colander so that excess liquid drains off.

Follow the same steps to roast thick slices of onion, unpeeled garlic cloves, husked tomatillos, or wedges of mango or pineapple. ***Onions*** should be roasted on both sides until softened, partially browned and fragrant. ***Garlic cloves*** should be watched carefully as they are easily scorched and will turn bitter. They should soften slightly. ***Tomatillos*** will turn soft, lose their shape and brown slightly. ***Pineapple and mango slices*** should brown slightly. Remember, you are adding flavor, not thoroughly cooking these ingredients.

RECONSTITUTING DRIED CHILES

Slit open the chile and remove the stem and however many seeds you want. With dried chipotles the stems can be more easily removed after soaking. The chiles will reconstitute quicker if you cut the two sides apart and separate them into two pieces. Put the dried chiles in a small, heat-resistant bowl, pour boiling water over them, and let them steep until they are pliable. Warning: Some of the capsaicin will rise in the steam and can briefly irritate your nose, throat and lungs. Try not to breathe in the steam. The water will leach some of the flavor out of dried chiles, so use as little water as possible, and leave them to steep for as short a time as necessary, usually 20 to 30 minutes. If the chiles are very dry and brittle, you can simmer them in water on the stovetop instead of steeping.

Process the chiles with their soaking water, fresh water or broth, as directed in the recipe. Strain to remove the bits of skin, if you wish. A good guideline is to strain the chiles if you are making a smooth sauce, but not to bother if they are going into a chunky salsa.

CHOPPING AND PROCESSING

The best uncooked salsa is made by hand, using a sharp knife. It is amazing how much faster and easier chopping is when your knives are well sharpened. Dull knives can bruise food, make cooking tedious, increase your chances of getting burned by the capsaicin in chiles, and prompt you to throw everything in the food processor. It is very tempting to do this anyway. A food processor chops and mixes everything in a few seconds, and you are less likely to burn your hands with capsaicin. It can also turn your salsa into a mushy blend that has lost the individual flavors of its ingredients. For this reason, it is best to use the food processor sparingly and carefully. So here are some rules to follow to help you if you absolutely must use the food processor – like when guests are expected in five minutes and you still haven't made the salsa.

1. Chop at least some of the ingredients by hand so that the salsa will have some texture. The food processor is best used for sturdier ingredients such as onions, garlic and roast chiles. Ingredients such as tomatoes and raw chiles have a higher proportion of water, and turn into a watery mess in the processor. Chop at least one tomato, and preferably all, by hand.

2. Use the processor's pulse button. It is better to process food in short bursts and check its consistency after each burst than to run it steadily until you have soup.

3. Add tomatoes after hardier items like onions are partially chopped. It takes longer to chop an onion in the food processor than it does to ruin tomatoes.

The rules change when you are making a cooked salsa and are looking for a smoother texture. Also, cooking will cause much of the watery liquid to evaporate. Again, however, you should use the processor sparingly, processing the salsa in short bursts rather than running it steadily.

The food processor is a useful tool when the primary ingredient in the salsa is roasted chiles or peppers. The roasting dries some of the water from the flesh and makes it sturdier. However, roast chiles can be a bit stringy, leaving you with long threads, even after processing. Cut roast chiles into strips across their width before putting them in the processor. This quick step avoids stringiness.

13

Serving spicy salsas at the Hatch Chile Festival. Wearing protective gloves like these helps to avoid the capsaicin in the chiles from burning your hands.

USEFUL TIPS

▶ If you are cooking salsa to reduce the liquid, use a wide, shallow pan rather than a deep saucepan. The liquid will boil off more quickly without overcooking the salsa.

▶ Allow uncooked salsas to sit for at least 30 minutes while the flavors meld, then taste and adjust the seasonings.

▶ To peel tomatoes, put them in a pot of boiling water for 30 to 40 seconds. The skins will slip off easily.

▶ Don't use aluminum pans or bowls. The acid in salsas will react with the metal and give the salsa a metallic taste.

uncooked salsas

Roast Jalapeño Salsa
Guacamole
Salsa Cruda I
Salsa Cruda II
Salsa Cruda III
Sweet Red Pepper Salsa
Cucumber Salsa
Corn Salsa
Zucchini Salsa

Avocado Salsa
Olive Salsa
Tomato-Mint Salsa
Tomatillo-Habanero Salsa
Spicy Herb Salsa
Cactus Salsa
Grilled Salsa
Black Bean Salsa
Cilantro-Chile Pesto
Kitchen Sink Guacamole
Radish Salsa
Roast Corn Salsa

Roast Jalapeño Salsa

Makes about 1½ cups

At first glance, this salsa may seem unbearably hot. But when the jalapeños are trimmed of seeds and veins, then roasted, they take on a wonderful mellow flavor that is only moderately spicy. Try this salsa on crackers, over steamed vegetables, or on meat or fish.

INGREDIENTS

15 jalapeño chiles
4 Anaheim chiles
3 ½-inch-thick slices of red onion, peeled
5 cloves garlic, unpeeled
¼ tsp dried oregano
2 tbsp olive oil
1 tbsp fresh lemon juice
¼ tsp salt

16

METHOD

► Cut the jalapeños and Anaheims in half, and remove the seeds and veins. Grill the chiles, onion slices and garlic over a barbecue kettle, or under a broiler, remembering to keep the skins of the chiles facing the heat source. The chiles will cook unevenly, and it's not necessary for the skins to be completely blackened. Don't cook them until they are charred through to the flesh. Remove them from the heat when they are ready and seal in a plastic bag or foil pouch. Leave them in the bag or pouch for 10 minutes. This will loosen the skins and make them easier to remove.

► The onion slices should soften and brown slightly. Turn and cook them on both sides. Turn the garlic once and cook until cloves are softened. Garlic will turn bitter if it is charred, so watch it closely.

► With a sharp knife, peel and scrape the skins off the chiles. Jalapeño skins are not as tough as many other chiles, so it's all right to leave part of the skin on. Roast chiles have a tendency to get stringy, so cut them in strips from side to side, not lengthwise. Put the strips in a food processor.

► Cut each onion slice into quarters and add them to the food processor. Peel the garlic, trim off any burned spots, and add that too. Add remaining ingredients and process until they are well chopped but not a paste. The mixture will be fairly dry.

GUACAMOLE

In its most primitive form, guacamole is nothing but mashed avocados and tomatoes. Most guacamoles and avocado salsas are a little more complex than that, but the best are made from a minimum of ingredients – avocados, onions, chiles, lime juice, salt and pepper.

That doesn't mean that a guacamole made with exotic ingredients is no good. Avocados go well with blue cheese, anchovies, and any number of other unorthodox additions. To prove it, there is a recipe for Kitchen Sink Guacamole on page 28, made with bacon and olives. Just don't let the wonderful flavor of a perfectly ripe avocado be overwhelmed by unnecessary ingredients.

Some tips for making guacamole and avocado salsas:

► Guacamole is supposed to be lumpy. Don't purée the avocados. Mash them with a fork, or use a hand mixer, but only briefly.

► Don't add the avocados until just before serving, or they will turn an unappetizing brown. That can be stalled by mixing the avocado chunks with lime juice, but not for long. Contrary to popular belief, putting an avocado pit in the guacamole will not keep it from turning brown.

► Buy hard avocados a few days before you plan to make guacamole, and let them ripen in a paper bag or on your kitchen counter, away from direct sunlight. If their flavor is still a little shy of perfection, mix in a few drops of avocado oil.

Guacamole

Makes about 2½ cups

This guacamole is made for chips, but it's also good on meat or taco salads. There is a little kick in the aftertaste from the hot pepper sauce, but it won't be very spicy unless you add some of the jalapeño seeds. I like my guacamole chunky, so I use a hand mixer rather than a food processor to blend the ingredients, then add some diced avocado afterwards for texture. You can prepare the other ingredients in advance, but don't add the avocado until just before serving.

Ingredients

2 avocados, peeled, pitted and diced
2 tomatoes, broiled, skinned and chopped
2 tbsp finely minced onion
2 cloves garlic, minced
2 jalapeño chiles, minced
1 tbsp olive oil
1 tbsp fresh lemon juice
dash of hot pepper sauce
salt and pepper to taste

Method

► Core the tomatoes, cut them in half and squeeze the seeds out. Place the tomatoes cut side down on a broiler-safe baking sheet and place them under the broiler. (*Note:* If the baking sheet does not have sides, line it with foil, then crimp the edges to form a shallow basin to catch the tomato juice.) Broil the tomatoes until the skin is just slightly blackened and loose. Slide off their skins, drain off excess juices, and let them cool.

► Using a hand mixer, combine about three-quarters of the diced avocado with all the remaining ingredients except salt and pepper. It should be slightly lumpy. Mix in the remaining avocado chunks, and add salt and pepper to taste. Serve immediately.

Clockwise from the top: Salsa Cruda I (page 18), Guacamole and Roast Jalapeño Salsa.

17

How Hot Is It?

How hot are these salsas? The answer is, as hot as you want them to be. The heat of a salsa depends not so much on how many chiles it contains, but on how they are cleaned and trimmed.

The heat of a chile comes from capsaicin, which is concentrated in the veins. Because the seeds are in contact with the veins, they taste hot too. If you trim all the seeds and veins from a chile it will be surprisingly mild.

Try this experiment: make two batches of any of the Salsa Cruda recipes. In one batch, trim away all the seeds and veins from the chiles. In the other, toss all the seeds and veins into the salsa. Now taste the difference.

After you have experimented with the seeds and veins, and know your preference, you can adjust all the salsa recipes in this book to your own preferred level of heat.

But what can you do when a salsa is too hot?

▶ Olive oil and puréed tomato can both help lower the heat of salsa by small degrees.

▶ If a salsa is way too hot, make a second batch, omitting the chiles, then combine the two batches.

▶ Dairy products such as sour cream can be mixed with salsa to combat the heat. The resulting salsa will have an entirely different character, but it will be far more tolerable.

Salsa Cruda I

Makes about 1½ cups

This is a basic tomato salsa, made with broiled or grilled tomatoes (see picture on page 17), and is good for dipping chips or spooning over egg dishes or tostadas.

It is pleasantly spicy rather than hot, but can be made more piquant if you don't trim away the jalapeño veins and seeds. It can be made several hours in advance.

Ingredients

3 large tomatoes, cored and halved
½ cup finely chopped onion
2 cloves garlic, minced
2 jalapeño chiles, seeded and minced
3 tbsp finely chopped cilantro
1 tbsp olive oil
1 tbsp fresh lime juice
salt to taste

Method

▶ Core the tomatoes, cut them in half and squeeze the seeds out. Place the tomatoes cut side down on a broiler-safe baking sheet and place them under the broiler. (*Note:* If the baking sheet does not have sides, line it with foil, then crimp the edges to form a shallow basin to catch the tomato juice.) Broil the tomatoes until the skin is just slightly blackened and loose. Slide off their skins, drain off excess juices, and let them cool.

▶ While the tomatoes are cooling, mix together all the remaining ingredients. Then chop the tomatoes and add them to the salsa. Let sit for 15 minutes or so, then taste and adjust the seasoning.

Salsa Cruda II

Makes 1 to 1½ cups

This version of Salsa Cruda has a lower proportion of tomatoes than the other two, and uses the hotter serrano chiles. It is an all-purpose salsa, good with chips, over tacos and tostadas, with meat and fish, or mixed into rice.

Ingredients

4 medium tomatoes, cored and halved
1 cup chopped onion
5 serrano chiles, partly seeded if desired, minced
2 cloves garlic, minced
3 tbsp chopped fresh cilantro
2 tbsp fresh lime juice
1 tbsp olive oil
¼ to ½ tsp salt

Method

▶ Cut the tomatoes in half and squeeze out seeds. Broil the tomatoes cut side down on a broiler-safe baking sheet until skins are partly blackened and skins slip off easily. Remove from heat. Let them cool in a colander so excess liquids drain off and then remove the skins. Purée in a blender or food processor, but do not purée so long that the tomato becomes liquefied.

▶ Stir all the remaining ingredients together and add the tomatoes. Let sit for 30 minutes, then taste and adjust the seasoning.

Salsa Cruda III

Clockwise from the top: Salsa Cruda III, Cucumber Salsa (page 20) and Sweet Red Pepper Salsa (page 20).

Makes 3 to 3½ cups salsa

The tomatoes are not broiled in this recipe, so the salsa is more chunky than soupy. It is good with chips, and can also be served as a topping for eggs, tostadas and soups, or mixed into vegetables. It is medium hot but can be made hotter by leaving in the jalapeño seeds.

INGREDIENTS

4 large tomatoes, seeded and chopped
½ cup chopped bell pepper
⅓ cup chopped red onion
⅓ cup chopped green onion
3 jalapeño chiles, seeded and chopped
3 tbsp chopped fresh cilantro
2 cloves garlic, minced
1 tbsp fresh lime juice
salt and pepper to taste

METHOD

▶ Combine all the ingredients. Let sit for about 15 minutes, then taste and adjust the salt and pepper. For a more liquid salsa, increase the amount of lime juice and/or add a little olive oil or other vegetable oil.

Sweet Red Pepper Salsa

Makes about 1½ cups

Roasted red bell peppers are the main ingredient in this versatile salsa (see picture on page 19), which has an unexpectedly sweet flavor. It is excellent with meat or fish, in an omelet, over pasta or steamed vegetables, or as a spread for crackers. For color, substitute yellow, orange or purple sweet peppers for some of the red.

INGREDIENTS

4 sweet red peppers
2 ½-inch-thick slices of onion, peeled
3 cloves garlic, unpeeled
2 serrano chiles, chopped and partly seeded
2 tbsp olive oil
1 tbsp chopped fresh basil or 1 tsp dried
1 tsp grated lemon rind
2 tbsp red wine vinegar
¼ tsp salt

METHOD

▶ To roast the red peppers, cut them into 4 or 5 pieces lengthwise so that they will lie relatively flat. Place the red peppers, onion slices and unpeeled garlic on a barbecue or under the broiler. The garlic should soften slightly, but needs to be watched closely as it scorches easily and turns bitter. The onions should be turned once, and should be softened and slightly browned. The skin of the red peppers should always face the heat source, and should be blistered and blackened, but take care not to char them so completely that the flesh is burned.

▶ Remove the peppers from the fire or the broiler as they blacken. They will probably cook unevenly. As you remove them, place them in a bag, a foil pouch, or a covered bowl. The steamy heat will loosen the skin and make it easy to remove after about 10 minutes.

▶ Pull the skin off the peppers. Because they have a tendency to get stringy lengthwise, cut them into several strips across their width. Peel the garlic cloves and trim off any scorched spots. Cut each onion slice into quarters. Put the peppers, onions, and garlic into a blender or food processor with the remaining ingredients. Process until the ingredients are well chopped but not so finely chopped that the salsa turns into a paste. Taste and adjust the seasoning.

20

Cucumber Salsa

Makes about 2½ cups

Radishes and cucumbers make this a crunchy salsa, good for topping soups and pozole (page 81), or as a dressing in a pita bread sandwich. With three jalapeños, it is moderately hot. See picture on page 19.

INGREDIENTS

1 small or ½ large cucumber, peeled, seeded and diced
2 large tomatoes, broiled (page 17) and chopped
3 jalapeño chiles, seeded and chopped
⅓ cup chopped radishes
½ cup chopped green onion
¼ cup chopped fresh cilantro
2 to 3 tbsp fresh lemon juice
2 to 3 tbsp vegetable oil
salt to taste

METHOD

▶ Combine all the ingredients except the salt. Let sit for about 15 minutes, then add salt to taste, and adjust the consistency by adding more lemon juice and oil, if necessary.

Corn Salsa

Makes about 2 cups

Made with garden-fresh vegetables, corn salsa is colorful and crunchy, and the jalapeños add gentle heat. For a spicier salsa, don't trim the veins and seeds from the jalapeños. Corn Salsa goes well with grilled seafood or as a garnish for soup. It's also the base for Corn Salsa Salad with Avocados (page 70). Use fresh corn whenever possible, but frozen corn can be substituted.

INGREDIENTS

1 cup corn kernels (1–2 ears)
3 tbsp diced sweet red pepper
3 tbsp diced bell pepper
2 jalapeño chiles, seeded and minced
¼ cup chopped green onions
1 large tomato, seeded and chopped
1 tbsp chopped fresh cilantro
2 tbsp olive oil
2 tbsp fresh lime juice
¼ tsp ground cumin
¼ tsp salt
pinch of black pepper

METHOD

▶ Put the corn in a small saucepan with ¼ cup boiling water. Cook just until tender, about 7 minutes. Drain the corn and let it cool. Meanwhile, combine all the remaining ingredients. Stir in the corn. Let sit for about 15 minutes for the flavors to blend, then taste and adjust the seasoning.

Zucchini Salsa

21

Makes about 2 cups

This spicy green relish is dominated by the flavor of cilantro, and goes well with roast or grilled meats. If you don't remove any seeds or veins from the jalapeño it will be fairly hot. It should be made no more than 24 hours before eating.

INGREDIENTS

2 cups shredded raw zucchini
⅓ cup finely chopped white onion
1 jalapeño chile, minced
⅓ cup chopped fresh cilantro
1 tbsp olive oil
1 tbsp rice vinegar
¼ tsp salt
1 tsp sugar

METHOD

▶ Mix all the ingredients together. Taste and adjust the seasoning.

Avocado Salsa

Makes about 2½ cups

What distinguishes Avocado Salsa from guacamole is that the avocado is chopped rather than mashed. This is a chunky, spicy salsa that is excellent, if a little messy, with chips. It is also delicious with grilled chicken or beef. Use avocados that are perfectly ripe, not the least bit overripe. If you want to prepare this salsa in advance, you may do so, but do not add the avocados until just before serving.

INGREDIENTS

2 large, ripe avocados, peeled, pitted
  and diced
3 tbsp fresh lime juice
1 tbsp olive oil
⅓ cup minced red onion
¼ cup diced sweet red pepper
3 jalapeño chiles, minced, some seeds
  included
¾ cup seeded and chopped tomato (about
  1 large)
1 tbsp chopped fresh cilantro
2 cloves garlic, minced
salt and pepper to taste

METHOD

▶ Mix the avocado chunks with the lime juice and olive oil, then stir in the remaining ingredients. Taste and adjust the seasoning.

22

Olive Salsa

Makes about 3 cups

Here's an unusual salsa that can be the star of a light meal, served over pasta. Try spooning it over salad, or spreading it on slices of French bread, too. There are a lot of strong flavors competing for attention, so the jalapeños won't even be noticeable if you don't include some seeds. If you dislike anchovies, they can be omitted.

INGREDIENTS

7-ounce jar of pitted green olives
3-ounce can of pitted black olives
3 cloves garlic, finely minced
2 jalapeño chiles, minced, some seeds
  included
⅓ cup finely chopped red onion
⅓ cup chopped sweet red pepper
2 ounces anchovy fillets (about 15), minced
¼ cup pine nuts, lightly toasted (see note
  below), then chopped
2 tbsp olive oil
1 tbsp red wine vinegar

METHOD

▶ Drain the olives and coarsely chop them. Mix them with all the remaining ingredients and let the flavors blend for at least 30 minutes before serving.

To toast pine nuts: Preheat the oven to 300°F. Spread the pine nuts in a single layer on a small baking sheet or a doubled sheet of aluminum foil. Bake for 5 to 10 minutes until they are lightly browned. Watch them closely, as they burn easily.

Avocado Salsa **(above)** *and Olive Salsa* **(below)**.

Tomato-Mint Salsa

Makes about 1½ cups

Mint gives an unusual flavor to this delicious salsa. It is good with fish, especially grilled fish, and also with meat.

INGREDIENTS

4 large tomatoes, cored, halved and seeded
2 cloves garlic, minced
1 tbsp olive oil
1 tbsp fresh lime juice
2 jalapeño chiles, with some seeds and
  veins, minced
¼ cup chopped fresh mint
¼ tsp salt
pinch of pepper

METHOD

▶ Halve the tomatoes and squeeze out the seeds. Broil or grill tomato halves, skin side towards the heat until the skin is partly blackened and slips off easily. Drain off any excess liquid. Chop the tomatoes in a food processor with the garlic, olive oil and lime juice, then stir in the jalapeños and mint. Add the salt and pepper, then taste and adjust the seasoning if necessary.

BONUSES

Looking for something to make your salsa snazzy? Here are a few additions that will go with most tomato salsas.

▶ ⅓ to ½ cup sliced black olives

▶ ⅓ cup finely diced jicama

▶ ½ to 1 cup sour cream

▶ 3 tablespoons beer

▶ a shot of tequila

24

Tomatillo-Habanero Salsa

Makes 1½ to 2 cups

Roasting the tomatillos and onions gives this salsa extra flavor, but it may be overwhelmed by the habanero chiles, one of the hottest chiles on earth. Fresh habaneros are hard to find, but you can substitute about 6 serrano or jalapeño chiles, unseeded. This salsa is good with chips, roast meat, or on Huevos Rancheros (page 127).

INGREDIENTS

8 tomatillos, husked and washed
1 small onion, peeled and cut into thick
  slices
4 cloves garlic, unpeeled
3 fresh habanero chiles, unseeded
¼ cup chopped fresh cilantro
1 tbsp fresh lime juice
1 tbsp olive oil
¼ tsp salt

METHOD

▶ Cut the tomatillos in half and roast them with the onion slices and garlic cloves over a barbecue fire. Alternatively, you can broil them, or brown them in a heavy, dry skillet. The tomatillos and onions should be lightly browned, and the garlic should be soft. Cool the garlic slightly, then peel it, cutting off any scorched parts as they will give the salsa a bitter flavor.

▶ Put the tomatillos, onion and garlic in a food processor with the remaining ingredients. Process until the mixture is chunky, not smooth. If the salsa is too dry, add a little more olive oil, lime juice or water.

Spicy Herb Salsa

Makes about 1½ cups

This salsa, inspired by Italian tomato sauces, uses fresh herbs to create a chunky, flavorful sauce that can be used as a dip, with meat, or over pastas or salads.

INGREDIENTS

¼ cup chopped fresh basil
1½ tsp chopped fresh oregano
½ tsp chopped fresh rosemary
5 cloves garlic, minced
2 tbsp olive oil
4 large tomatoes, seeded and diced
½ cup chopped onion
2 jalapeño chiles, partially seeded, minced
2 tbsp red wine vinegar
¼ tsp salt

METHOD

▶ If you can start this salsa in advance, mix the fresh herbs, garlic, and olive oil, and let steep for at least an hour. Then combine with the remaining ingredients. Otherwise, combine all the ingredients at once, but let the flavors meld for at least 30 minutes before serving. Taste and adjust the salt.

Cactus Salsa

25

Makes about 2½ cups

In Mexico and the southwestern United States, broad, flat cactus paddles are cleaned, cooked and eaten as an ingredient in a number of dishes. Bottled nopales can be found in the Mexican food section of many grocery stores. In this recipe, the hot flavor provided by unseeded jalapeños provides a counterpoint to the mild nopales. Use as a dip for chips, or mix it into scrambled eggs.

INGREDIENTS

4 large tomatoes, halved and seeded
11-ounce jar of nopales, chopped (about 1 cup)
¼ cup chopped green onion
⅓ cup chopped white onion
3 jalapeño chiles, unseeded, chopped
3 tbsp chopped fresh cilantro
1 tbsp red wine vinegar
1 tbsp fresh lime juice
1 tbsp olive oil
salt and pepper to taste

METHOD

▶ Cut the tomatoes in half and squeeze out the seeds. Cook them under the broiler or on a barbecue grill, skins towards the heat, until the skins blacken and slip off easily. Let the tomatoes cool slightly, remove the skins and chop them. Mix with the remaining ingredients. Let sit for 30 minutes, then taste and adjust the seasoning.

Chile plants growing in the fields of New Mexico.

Grilled Salsa

Makes about 2 cups

All the main ingredients in this salsa are grilled, giving it a delicious smoky taste. The poblano chiles add mild to moderate heat. A grilling tray for small items is a necessity or you'll lose the garlic and most of the tomato in the coals. If you don't have a tray, you may broil the vegetables rather than grill them, but the flavor will not be as good. Remember to keep the skins of the tomatoes and chiles facing the heat source.

INGREDIENTS

5 large tomatoes, halved and seeded
1 small white onion, peeled and cut into
*   thick slices*
3 poblano chiles, quartered lengthwise
4 cloves garlic, unpeeled
1 tbsp fresh lime juice
salt and pepper to taste

METHOD

▶ Halve the tomatoes and place them, cut side up, on a grilling tray. Add the chiles skin side down. It doesn't matter which way you turn the onion and garlic. When the barbecue flames have died down and the coals are glowing, place the tray of vegetables directly over the coals.

▶ Turn the garlic frequently and remove it as soon as it softens, as it will turn bitter and mar the taste of the salsa if it scorches. When the garlic is cooked enough to handle, peel it.

▶ The skin on the chiles should brown and blister, but the flesh must not burn. Don't expect the skin to blister evenly. As soon as each piece of chile is done, put it in a plastic bag and close the top.

▶ The onion slices should brown slightly. Then turn them over and let the other side brown. Again, don't let them burn.

▶ Cook the tomatoes until the skin browns and slides off easily. It's fine if the flesh browns a little. When the tomatoes are cooked, put them in a bowl or colander where liquid can drain off.

▶ Allow the chiles to steam in the bag for about 10 minutes. Then with a sharp knife, peel off the blistered skin. It's okay if a few bits of charred skin remain. Because poblanos have a tendency to get stringy, cut each piece into a few short pieces.

▶ Put chiles, peeled garlic, onion slices and drained tomatoes in a blender or food processor with lime juice and a little salt and pepper. Process until the vegetables are well chopped, but not to the point where the mixture is completely smooth. Taste and adjust the salt and pepper.

Black Bean Salsa

Makes about 2 cups

Black Bean Salsa has an excellent mixture of textures and flavors, producing a spicy relish that goes well with fish, meat, and eggs. You may use canned black beans (a 1-pound can is approximately 1¼ cups of cooked beans) or soak and cook dried beans. You can also use kidney beans. With canned beans, this is a very easy-to-make dish.

INGREDIENTS

1-pound can of black or kidney beans, rinsed
*   and drained*
⅓ cup chopped sweet red pepper
3 green onions, chopped
2 chipotle chiles, minced
3 tbsp chopped fresh cilantro
1½ tsp chopped fresh oregano or ½ tsp dried
1 tbsp olive oil
2 tbsp fresh lime juice
salt to taste

METHOD

▶ Combine all the ingredients. Let sit for about 30 minutes, then taste and adjust the seasoning.

Grilled Salsa (above) and Black Bean Salsa (below).

Cilantro-Chile Pesto

Makes about 1½ cups

This spicy pesto uses traditional salsa ingredients, although its texture is different. It is simple and delicious. Spoon it over pasta, steamed vegetables or meat.

INGREDIENTS

1½ cups fresh cilantro leaves, quite tightly packed
5 cloves garlic, peeled
1 jalapeño chile
2 poblano chiles, broiled (page 12) and peeled
½ large red onion
½ cup olive oil
½ cup walnuts
½ tsp salt

METHOD

▶ Put all the ingredients in a food processor and process until almost smooth.

Kitchen Sink Guacamole

28

Makes about 3 cups

This guacamole is a purist's nightmare, but never mind, it has a great taste.

INGREDIENTS

3 large avocados, crudely mashed (but not puréed)
2 tomatoes, seeded and chopped
¼ cup chopped onion
2 jalapeño chiles, chopped and partly seeded
2 tbsp fresh lime juice
6 slices bacon, cooked and crumbled
¼ cup sliced black olives
salt and pepper to taste

METHOD

▶ Combine all the ingredients, then taste and adjust the seasoning. Serve immediately.

Radish Salsa

Makes about 2 cups

Serve this hot radish relish as a side dish with grilled meats, especially pork.

INGREDIENTS

¼ cup finely chopped red onion
1½ tsp crushed dried chile
⅓ cup white wine vinegar
2 cups thinly sliced radishes (about 2 bunches)
3 tbsp chopped fresh cilantro
1 tbsp olive oil
pinch of salt

METHOD

▶ Combine the onion, chile and vinegar, and let steep for at least 1 hour. Mix in the remaining ingredients.

Roast Corn Salsa

Makes about 3 cups

Because some of the vegetables are grilled, this sauce has a smoky flavor and a very different texture from the preceding Corn Salsa. It is a more sophisticated recipe that goes well with grilled chicken and meat, and is also the base for a delicious crab chowder (page 78). Without jalapeño seeds, it is moderately spicy.

INGREDIENTS

4 large ears of corn, in husks
3 large tomatoes
1 poblano chile
2 cloves garlic, unpeeled
½ sweet red pepper
½ cup chopped green onions
2 jalapeño chiles, seeded and minced
2 tbsp chopped fresh cilantro
1 tsp chopped fresh oregano or ¼ tsp dried
3 tbsp olive oil
salt and pepper to taste

METHOD

▶ Carefully peel the corn husks back and remove the silks. Pull the husks back up and tie at the top with string if necessary. Soak the corn in water for 30 minutes, then drain, place in a 400°F oven, and roast for 20 minutes. Leave until cool enough to handle.

▶ While corn is cooling, preheat the broiler. Core the tomatoes, cut them in half and squeeze out the seeds. Place them cut side down on a broiler-safe baking sheet.

▶ Cut the poblano chile in quarters lengthwise, removing the stem, veins and seeds. Cut the half of the sweet red pepper in half again lengthwise. Place the chile and the red pepper on the baking sheet, skin side up. If the chile or pepper pieces don't lie nearly flat, cut them into additional pieces so that the skin is fairly evenly exposed to the broiler. Put the unpeeled garlic cloves on the baking sheet too. The ingredients will cook at different speeds, so watch them carefully, moving them as needed.

▶ The tomato skin should darken and loosen enough so that it will slip off easily. The skin

on the poblano chile and the red pepper should be almost completely blackened. The garlic cloves should soften. Remove each piece when it is ready. Place the chile and the pepper into a plastic bag or make a foil pouch. After 10 minutes, remove the chile and pepper from the bag and cut off the blackened skin, leaving just a few bits of skin on the flesh for color and flavor. Slip the skins off the tomatoes and drain off the excess juices. Peel the garlic cloves. Chop the tomatoes, chile, red pepper and garlic, and put them in a medium bowl.

▶ Remove the husks from the corn and roast the ears over glowing coals or under a broiler. Turn them frequently so that bits of the kernels are browned on all sides. Do not allow the corn to brown completely.

▶ Remove the corn from the grill or broiler and leave until cool enough to handle. With a sharp knife, cut the kernels off the cobs and add to the vegetables. Stir in the green onions, jalapeños, cilantro, oregano, olive oil, salt and pepper. Taste and adjust the seasoning.

29

In this mass of red and green chiles you can see how the chiles ripen from green through to red.

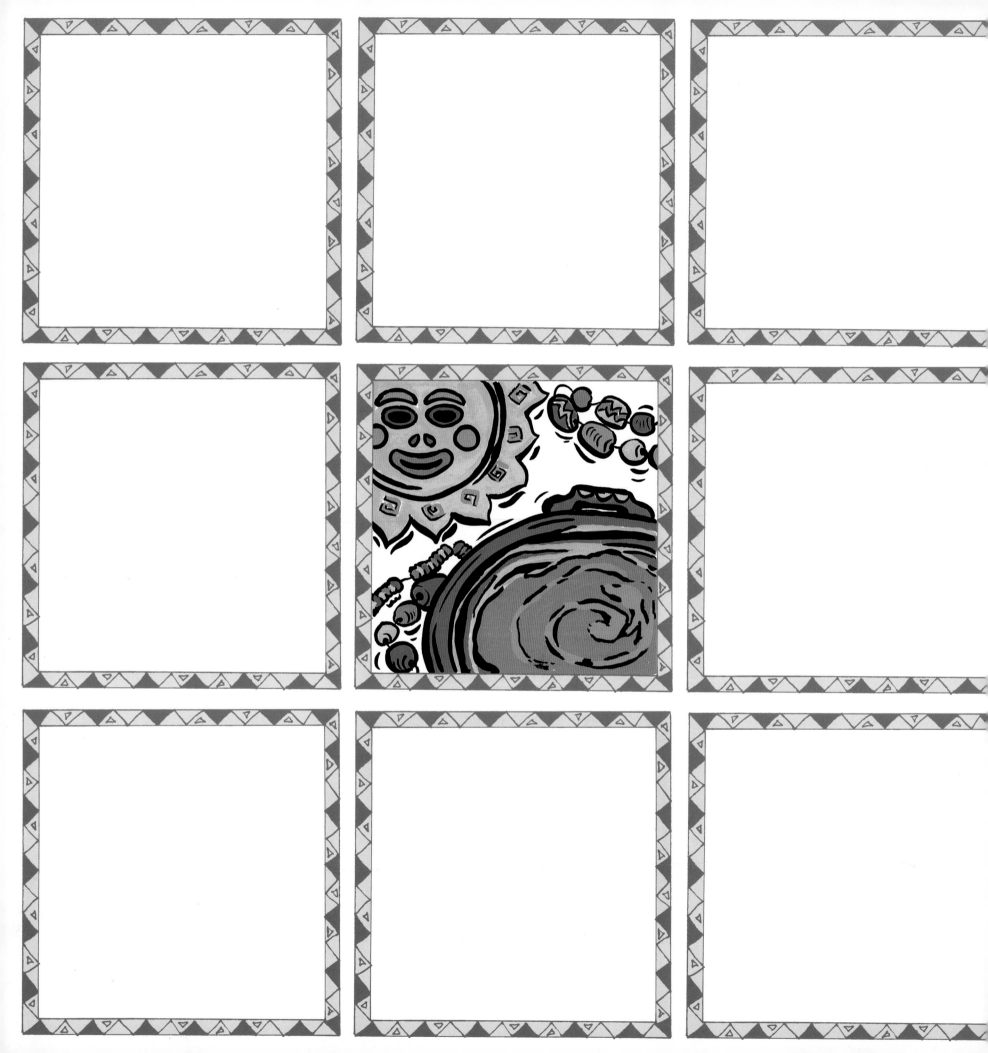

cooked salsas

Basic Cooked Salsa

Makes 2 to 2½ cups

This simple cooked salsa is good with chips or as a sauce over eggs or Mexican food. With a few jalapeño seeds included, it is fairly hot. You may use unpeeled tomatoes, but if you wish to remove the skin, dip the tomatoes in boiling water for 30 seconds. The skins should slip off easily.

INGREDIENTS

2 cups seeded, chopped tomatoes
2 cloves minced garlic
½ cup finely chopped onion
4 jalapeño chiles, chopped, with some seeds included
1 tbsp cider vinegar
1 tsp fresh oregano or ¼ tsp dried
salt to taste

METHOD

▶ In a medium saucepan, simmer the tomatoes, garlic and onion for 10 to 15 minutes, uncovered, to evaporate excess liquid from the tomatoes. Add the jalapeños, vinegar and oregano, and simmer for 5 minutes more. Add salt to taste.

Green Chile Sauce

32

Makes about 2 cups

This delicious sauce is traditionally made with green New Mexico chiles. However, since fresh New Mexico chiles are hard to find much of the year, you can substitute mild Anaheim chiles and add several jalapeño or serrano chiles to boost the heat. This sauce is a key ingredient in enchiladas, but can also be served with tacos, chips, and many other dishes.

INGREDIENTS

6 green New Mexico chiles (or 6 Anaheim chiles plus 3 to 4 jalapeño or serrano chiles)
3 cloves garlic
4 tomatillos, husked and halved
2 ½-inch-thick slices of white onion, peeled
¼ tsp salt
1 cup water or chicken broth

METHOD

▶ Roast the chiles, garlic, tomatillos and onion as described on page 26 under Grilled Salsa. Peel and seed the chiles, and cut them into strips across their width. Peel the garlic. Cut the tomatillos and onions into chunks. Purée the chiles, garlic, tomatillos and onion with the salt and ½ cup water or chicken broth. Put the purée in a saucepan with the remaining water or broth and simmer until it reaches the desired consistency. Taste and adjust the salt.

The warm color of red chiles lends a wonderful richness to sauces.

Red Chile Sauce

Makes 2 to 2½ cups

This hot chile sauce is used most often to make enchiladas, but it can also be added to meat or beans, or served as a table sauce to be spooned over tacos, eggs, or other dishes. For less heat, substitute dried California chiles for some of the New Mexico chiles. Or for variety, use a combination of New Mexico, California, ancho, or other dried chiles.

INGREDIENTS

12 dried New Mexico chiles
2½ cups beef broth
4 cloves garlic, minced
½ cup chopped onion
½ tsp dried oregano
¼ tsp salt

METHOD

▶ Preheat the oven to 250°F. Place the chiles on an ungreased baking sheet and bake for 6 to 8 minutes, shaking once or twice, until they are brittle. Do not allow them to blacken or they will be bitter. Remove the chiles and let sit until they are cool enough to handle. Remove the stems and as many of the seeds as desired.

▶ Bring 1 quart water to a boil in a medium saucepan. Crumble the chiles into the boiling water and simmer for 20 to 30 minutes until soft. Drain off the water and discard. Put the chiles into a food processor with about ½ cup of the beef broth and purée. Strain to remove the skins. Put the skins back in the food processor with another ½ cup beef broth. Purée again and strain. Discard the skins.

▶ Add the remaining ingredients to the strained sauce and purée. Return the sauce to the heat, and simmer until it reaches the desired consistency.

Clockwise from the top: *Basic Cooked Salsa, Green Chile Sauce and Red Chile Sauce.*

Chipotle Salsa

Makes about 2 cups

This hot, smoky salsa gets its marvelous flavor from dried chipotle chiles. It is excellent with chips, on Huevos Rancheros (page 127), tacos or with meat.

INGREDIENTS

4 dried chipotle chiles
2 cups seeded and chopped tomatoes
1/2 cup chopped onion
1/2 cup chopped bell pepper
salt to taste

METHOD

▶ Remove the seeds and stems, and put the chipotle chiles in a small, heat-resistant bowl and pour 2/3 cup boiling water over them. Let them soak until they are pliable, about 30 minutes. If chiles are very dry and brittle, gently simmer them in the water. Remove the stems, then put the chiles and the soaking water in a food processor and purée.

▶ Put the chipotle purée in a small saucepan with all the remaining ingredients. Simmer until any excess liquid evaporates, 15 to 20 minutes. If the chipotles did not purée easily, or if you want a smooth sauce for dipping, briefly process the salsa again.

Note: You may also use chipotle chiles canned in adobo sauce. Skip the steeping in hot water. Coarsely chop the chipotles before adding them to the salsa, then process after the salsa is cooked. Without the soaking water, there will not be as much excess liquid, and the salsa will not have to cook quite as long.

34

Salsa Verde

Makes about 2 cups

Fresh tomatillos give Salsa Verde its green color. It tastes best when it is very spicy, so include the jalapeño seeds and veins. Use as you would a basic tomato salsa.

INGREDIENTS

1 pound tomatillos (about 20), husked and washed
2 jalapeño chiles, unseeded, chopped
1 clove garlic, minced
1 medium onion, chopped
¼ cup chopped fresh cilantro
1 tbsp fresh lemon juice
½ tsp salt
1 to 2 tbsp vegetable oil
1 to 2 tsp sugar (optional)

METHOD

▶ Add the tomatillos to a pan of boiling water and simmer for 10 minutes. Drain, and transfer to a blender or food processor. Process until finely chopped.

▶ Mix all the remaining ingredients except the oil and sugar with the tomatillos. Heat the oil in a skillet, add the salsa and fry briefly, then simmer until the excess liquid has reduced, about 10 minutes. Taste. If the tomatillos were too green and the salsa is tart, add the sugar.

Garlic Salsa

3 5

Makes 1 to 1½ cups

Use this pungent sauce as you would any other tomato-based salsa – with chips, over eggs, on tacos, or with meat.

INGREDIENTS

3 large tomatoes, peeled, seeded and diced
½ cup chopped onion
1 japaleño chile, trimmed of all but a few seeds and veins
¼ to ½ tsp salt
12 cloves garlic, minced
1 tbsp chopped fresh basil or 1 tsp dried

METHOD

▶ Simmer the tomatoes, onion, jalapeño and ¼ tsp salt for about 10 minutes to evaporate excess liquid. Add the garlic and basil, and cook for another 2 to 3 minutes. Taste and adjust the salt if necessary.

Black Bean-Corn Salsa

Makes 5 to 6 cups

Made with roasted corn and three kinds of chiles, this is a hearty salsa that fills your mouth with a symphony of flavors. It is delicious warm with grilled salmon. Serve it on the side or as a topping for other fish, chicken or pork, or as a vegetarian main dish. In a pinch, you can substitute 2 cups of canned black beans, rinsed and drained, but there is no doubt that the warm, cooked dried beans have a better flavor.

INGREDIENTS

1 cup dried black beans
3 large ears of corn or 5 small ears, still in
  their husks
1 small onion, peeled and quartered
4 cloves garlic
2 ancho chiles, halved and seeded
2 large tomatoes, cored, halved and seeded
2 Anaheim chiles, halved and seeded
½ cup chopped red onion
½ cup chopped green onion
2 jalapeño chiles, seeded and minced
1 tsp cumin
1 to 3 tsp salt

36

METHOD

▶ Sort the dried beans, removing any pebbles. Put the beans in a medium saucepan and add 3 cups of water. Bring to a boil and boil for 2 minutes, then cover the pan, turn off the heat and let sit for 1 hour.

▶ Meanwhile, prepare the corn. Carefully peel back the husks and remove the silks, then pull the husks back up around the corn. Soak the corn in cool water for 30 minutes. If you are going to grill the corn, start a charcoal fire in the barbecue.

▶ Drain and rinse the beans. Put them in a large saucepan, add 3 cups water, the quartered onion and 2 cloves garlic, peeled and crushed. Bring to a boil, reduce the heat and simmer, uncovered, until the beans are tender and the liquid has evaporated, 1 to 1½ hours. Check occasionally, adding more water if needed.

▶ While the beans are cooking, prepare the ancho chiles and roast the vegetables. Reconstitute the ancho chile halves in ⅓ cup boiling water in a small, heat-resistant bowl. Leave to soak for 20 minutes, stirring once or twice to be sure all of the chile is softened. Purée the chiles and their soaking liquid in a blender, then add this purée to the beans while they are simmering.

▶ Drain the corn. If you are using a barbecue, the coals should be glowing, and no longer flaming. Add a few more coals to extend the barbecuing time, then place the corn at the side of the barbecue grill, not directly over the coals. Cover the grill and let the corn roast for 20 minutes. Alternatively, place the corn on a baking pan and cook in a preheated 400° oven for 20 minutes. Remove the corn and leave until cool enough to handle. If you are using the oven, turn on the broiler. Remove the husks from the corn and

place the corn on the grill over the coals, or under the broiler, turning so that the kernels are lightly browned in spots. Do not let it brown all over or it will be too dry. Remove from the heat and let sit until cool enough to handle. Cut the kernels from the cobs.

▶ Roast the tomatoes and Anaheim chiles on the grill over charcoal or under the broiler. Always make sure the skins face the heat source. Cook until tomato skins are browned and slip off easily, and until chile skins are almost completely blackened. Put the chiles in a small bag or in an envelope of aluminum foil for 10 minutes. Remove the skin from the chiles (it's fine if you leave a little bit of blackened skin on) and slip the skin from the tomatoes. Chop the tomatoes and chiles.

▶ Remove the beans from the heat, discarding the onion and garlic. Mince the remaining 2 cloves garlic and add to the beans with the roast corn, chopped tomatoes and Anaheim chiles. Stir in the remaining ingredients, including 1 tsp salt. Taste and add more salt if needed. Serve warm or at room temperature.

Clockwise from the top: Black Bean-Corn Salsa, Fiery Habanero Salsa (page 38) and Winter Salsa I (page 38).

Fiery Habanero Salsa

Makes about 1 cup

This salsa, which uses a single dried habanero chile, is the hottest in the book, and tolerable only to those whose nerve endings are already irreparably damaged by capsaicin. It is excellent with almost everything – chips, eggs, meat or tacos. Just be sure to have lots of milk available for relief. See picture on page 37.

INGREDIENTS

1 whole dried habanero chile
1 cup tomatoes, skinned, seeded and chopped
1/2 cup chopped red onion
2 cloves garlic, minced
1/4 cup chopped fresh cilantro
1 tbsp cider vinegar
1 tbsp olive oil
1/4 tsp salt

METHOD

► Remove and discard the stem of the habanero and then reconstitute it in ⅔ cup boiling water for about 30 minutes. Then chop coarsely. Put the habanero and its soaking water in a small saucepan with the tomato, onion and garlic. Simmer for 10 to 15 minutes, until the excess liquid has evaporated. Add all the remaining ingredients and cook for 2 minutes longer. Put the salsa in a food processor or blender and process until the habanero is well chopped, but the salsa is not completely puréed.

38

Winter Salsa I

OUT-OF-SEASON SALSA

So it's January and you have a craving for salsa and chips, but the only tomatoes in the store are hard and flavorless. As for fresh chiles, there are none. Don't worry; you can still satisfy that craving.

Canned tomatoes, especially Italian plum tomatoes, are better than unripe fresh tomatoes. Canned chiles are not a good substitute for fresh ones – unless they are chipotle chiles – but dried chiles are.

The next three recipes for salsa use ingredients that can be found in the grocery store year-round. You won't mistake them for Salsa Cruda, but they're good. See page 24 for additions that will give your salsa an extra snap.

Makes 1½ to 2 cups

This moderately spicy pantry salsa (see picture on page 37) is based on canned tomatoes and dried ancho chiles, making it suitable for the winter months when good, flavorsome, fresh ingredients are hard to come by. Serve with chips, on tacos and other tortilla dishes, or with eggs.

INGREDIENTS

2 ancho chiles (sometimes labeled pasillas)
14½-ounce can of whole tomatoes
2 cloves garlic, minced
1/2 cup chopped onion
2 to 3 tsp dried cilantro
1 tsp sugar
1/4 tsp salt

METHOD

► Cut open the ancho chiles and remove the stems and most of the seeds. Cut the chiles into 1-inch pieces – this will make it easier to process the salsa. Put the chile pieces in a small, heat-resistant bowl and pour a half-cup or more of boiling water over the chiles. Use as little water as possible, and stir to be sure all the pieces are covered with water. Let them sit for 20 minutes, or longer if the chiles seem particularly dry.

► Drain the chiles, discarding the water. Put the chile pieces in a blender or food processor with about half the tomatoes and their juice. Process until the chiles are well chopped. Chop the remaining tomatoes by hand and put in a small saucepan with the chile mixture and the remaining ingredients. Simmer for 10 minutes or so until the excess liquid has evaporated.

Winter Salsa II

Makes about 1½ cups

Canned tomatoes and chipotle chiles are the main ingredients of this hot, smoky salsa. The chiles are canned in adobo sauce, some of which is added to the salsa.

INGREDIENTS

14½-ounce can of whole or chopped (not stewed) tomatoes
3 chipotle chiles canned in adobo sauce, plus 1 tbsp adobo sauce
½ cup chopped onion
½ tsp dried oregano
salt to taste

METHOD

▶ Process the tomatoes, chipotle chiles and adobo sauce in a food processor, leaving the mixture a little chunky. Put the salsa in a small saucepan and add the onions and oregano. Simmer for 10 minutes, then add salt to taste.

Winter Salsa III

Makes about 1 cup

This fiery New Mexico salsa uses crushed dried chiles to give it its heat. Add another tablespoon of chili flakes to make it even hotter.

INGREDIENTS

¼ cup chopped onion
2 tbsp red chile flakes
1 tsp dried oregano
⅓ cup red wine vinegar
14½-ounce can of whole tomatoes
¼ tsp ground cumin
¼ to ½ tsp salt

METHOD

▶ Combine the onion, chili flakes, oregano and vinegar. Let the mixture steep for at least an hour. Chop, but don't completely purée, the tomatoes in a blender or food processor. Put the tomatoes in a small saucepan with the vinegar mixture, cumin and salt. Bring to a boil and simmer for 10 minutes, or longer if needed, to reduce the excess liquid. Taste and adjust the seasoning.

39

In certain parts of America, the chile crop is celebrated each year with festivals, parades and cook-offs.

fruit
salsas

Avocado-Mango Salsa
Pineapple-Ginger Salsa
Tropical Salsa
Grilled Mango-Habanero Salsa
Cranberry-Papaya Salsa
Nectarine Salsa
Jicama-Peach Salsa
Mango Salsa
Black Bean-Papaya Salsa

Avocado-Mango Salsa

Makes about 2 cups

The rich, pleasantly sweet combination of avocado and mango is made piquant with hot serrano chiles and red onion. Serve with meat, poultry or fish.

INGREDIENTS

1 mango, peeled, pitted and diced
1 avocado, peeled, pitted and diced
2 serrano chiles, unseeded, minced
1/2 cup chopped red onion
3 tbsp chopped fresh cilantro
2 tbsp fresh lime juice
2 tbsp orange juice
pinch of ground cumin

METHOD

▶ Combine all the ingredients.

Pineapple-Ginger Salsa

Makes about 3 cups

42

Grilling the pineapple mellows its acidity and provides a sweet counterpoint to the sharp kick of jalapeño and fresh ginger. This salsa goes well with meat, especially pork, but it's so good you may just want to eat it straight from the bowl. It should be eaten the same day it is prepared.

INGREDIENTS

2 or 3 1-inch thick slices of fresh pineapple, unpeeled
1/2 cup chopped sweet red pepper
1/2 cup chopped red onion
2 jalapeño chiles, unseeded, chopped
2 to 3 tsp finely minced fresh ginger
1 tbsp rice vinegar

METHOD

▶ Grill the pineapple slices over glowing embers until they are marked with brown lines from the grill and show spots of brown, 3 to 5 minutes a side. Let the pineapple cool slightly, then pare off the peel and cut out the tough core. Dice the flesh to make 2 cups of pineapple. Mix with the remaining ingredients. Let sit for at least 30 minutes to allow the flavors to blend.

Tropical Salsa

Makes 1½ to 2 cups

There's a definite whiff of the tropics in this salsa, which includes mango, pineapple and mint. Make it no more than a few hours before you plan to eat, and serve it as an accompaniment to meat. I use it to dress up plain roast turkey.

INGREDIENTS

1 ripe mango, peeled, pitted and diced
1/2 cup fresh pineapple, peeled and diced
2 tbsp chopped fresh mint
2 tbsp chopped fresh cilantro
1/4 cup chopped red onion
1 serrano chile, minced
1 sweet Italian or other mild chile, seeded and minced
1 tbsp orange juice
1 tbsp olive oil
1/4 to 1/2 tsp ground cumin
salt to taste

METHOD

▶ Combine all the ingredients. Let sit for at least 20 minutes, then taste and adjust the seasoning if necessary.

Clockwise from the top: Avocado-Mango Salsa, Tropical Salsa and Pineapple-Ginger Salsa.

Grilled Mango-Habanero Salsa

Makes 1½ to 2 cups

This sweet-hot salsa, which goes well with meat or poultry, is an unusual combination of grilled mango, sweet onions, and fiery habanero chiles. Grilling intensifies the sweetness of the mango, which decreases the habanero's fire. It is only moderately hot if you remove the veins and seeds from the habanero, but incendiary if you leave them in. If you cannot find habanero chiles, substitute 3 serrano chiles. It is important to use a special grilling tray, otherwise, you will almost certainly lose some of the mango in the barbecue coals.

INGREDIENTS

2 ripe but firm mangoes
1 large or 2 small Vidalia or other
sweet onions
1 habanero chile, minced
3 tbsp minced fresh cilantro
2 tbsp fresh lime juice
1 tbsp rice vinegar
pinch of salt

METHOD

► Cut the mangoes into wedges but do not peel them, because the rind will make them easier to handle as they soften during grilling.

Peel and cut a large onion into thick slices, or cut small onions in half. Put the mangoes and onions on a lightly oiled grilling tray, and cook until a few brown spots appear on the mango flesh. Turn the mangoes. The onions should be turned when they are a little browner than the mangoes, but not completely brown. Remove and let cool.

► Cut the rind off the mango slices and cut the flesh into ¼-inch dice. The fruit should be very juicy. Chop the grilled onions and add to the mangoes with the remaining ingredients.

44

Cranberry-Papaya Salsa

Makes about 2 cups

Here's a spicy twist on the traditional cranberry sauce served with holiday roast turkey. Two unseeded jalapeño chiles give it an unexpected bite. With slight adjustments, this salsa can be served cooked or raw. For a sharper, rough-textured relish, serve it raw. The cooked version is sweeter and smoother.

INGREDIENTS

½ orange, unpeeled
½ medium onion, peeled
2 jalapeño chiles, stems removed, unseeded
3 cups fresh or frozen cranberries
1 tbsp fresh lime juice
¼ cup honey
1 papaya, peeled, seeded and cut into
¼-inch dice

UNCOOKED SALSA

► Cut the orange and onion halves into a few chunks, and remove the orange seeds. Put the orange and onion in a food processor and chop coarsely. Cut the jalapeños into 3 or 4 pieces and add them to the orange and onion, together with the cranberries, lime juice and honey. Process until well chopped. Do not process so long that the salsa becomes liquefied or turns into a paste. Remove from the processor and mix with the papaya. Taste and adjust the lime juice and honey, if needed.

COOKED SALSA

Ingredients as listed but with:
⅓ cup honey
2 tbsp water

► Cut and process the orange and onion as directed above. Add the cranberries, lime juice, honey and water. Do not add the jalapeños. Process, then transfer to a small saucepan and simmer for about 10 minutes, until the water has evaporated and the sauce is ruby-colored. Check the sweetness, and add more honey, if desired. Remove from the heat and let cool. Mince the jalapeños and add to the cooked salsa with the papaya.

Nectarine Salsa

Makes about 1 cup

Sweet nectarines are mixed with onion and fresh chile, then sprinkled with chili powder to make a spicy-sweet salsa that is delicious with seafood or chicken. It can be made several hours in advance.

INGREDIENTS

3 ripe nectarines, peeled, pitted and chopped
4 tbsp finely chopped green onion
1 jalapeño or serrano chile, finely chopped,
some seeds included
¼ cup finely chopped sweet red pepper
2 tbsp chopped fresh basil
2 tbsp fresh lime juice
¼ tsp chili powder
salt and pepper to taste

METHOD

▶ With a fork, mash about 2 tablespoons of the chopped nectarine. Stir in the rest of the nectarine and the remaining ingredients. Let sit for about 15 minutes, then taste and adjust the seasoning.

Jicama-Peach Salsa

Makes about 2½ cups

45

Jicama-Peach Salsa is sweet, moderately hot and crunchy. It makes an excellent side dish.

INGREDIENTS

1 cup finely diced jicama (about ½ medium jicama, peeled)
⅔ cup chopped red onion
⅓ cup chopped sweet red pepper
2 medium peaches, peeled, pitted and chopped
2 jalapeño chiles, unseeded, chopped

2 to 3 tbsp fresh lime juice
½ tsp chili powder
1 tbsp chopped fresh basil

METHOD

▶ Combine all the ingredients.

Fresh fruits and vegetables combine well with the spicy tastes of chiles in salsas.

Mango Salsa

Makes just under 2 cups

Mango is a popular ingredient in salsas from the Caribbean and the Philippines because its cool sweetness provides a perfect complement to the spiciness of the chiles.

INGREDIENTS

2 mangoes, peeled, pitted and diced
½ cup chopped red onion
½ cup chopped sweet red pepper
2 jalapeño chiles, seeded and chopped
3 tbsp fresh lime juice

METHOD

▶ Combine all the ingredients.

Black Bean-Papaya Salsa

Makes about 2½ cups

This beautiful, spicy-sweet salsa is spiked with fresh ginger. It goes well with chicken, fish and meat, especially pork.

INGREDIENTS

1-pound can of black beans, rinsed and
*   drained*
1 papaya, peeled, seeded and diced
2 poblano chiles, roasted (page 12),
*   peeled and chopped*
½ cup sweet red pepper, chopped
½ cup chopped red onion
¼ cup chopped fresh cilantro
1 tsp finely minced fresh ginger
¼ cup fresh lime juice
1 tsp crushed dried red chile
salt and pepper to taste

METHOD

▶ Combine all the ingredients. Let sit for 30 minutes, then taste and adjust the seasoning.

46

Black Bean-Papaya Salsa **(above)** *and Mango Salsa* **(below)**.

appetizers

Triple-Treat Salsa Spread
Prosciutto Shrimp
Hot Bean Dip
Chorizo-Bean Dip
Chicken-Avocado Salsa Spread
Nachos
Layered Fiesta Dip
Seafood Salsa Spread
Homemade Tortilla Chips
Empanadas

Chile con Queso
Tostaditas

Triple-Treat Salsa Spread

Makes 3 to 3½ cups

This party dish incorporates three different salsas and cream cheese into a layered spread that is absolutely delicious. It should be made at least 4 hours in advance of serving, and improves if prepared 24 hours in advance. It is easier to make if you chill the spread for about 30 minutes after adding each layer. For a simpler dish, you can omit the Avocado Salsa, or spoon more tomato salsa over the top instead. Serve it with crackers.

INGREDIENTS

1 pound cream cheese
2 tbsp milk
⅓ cup tomato-based salsa, such as Basic
*   Cooked Salsa (page 32)*
1 cup Cilantro-Chile Pesto (page 28)
1 to 1½ cups Avocado Salsa (page 22)

50

METHOD

► Select a straight-sided or nearly straight-sided dish that is 5 to 6 inches in diameter and at least 2 inches deep; a soufflé dish is perfect. Line the bottom and sides with plastic wrap, smoothing out the plastic as much as possible. Leave some plastic wrap overhanging the sides of the dish.

► Beat half the cream cheese with the milk so it is easily spreadable but not runny. Spread this mixture as evenly as possible over the bottom of the dish. Chill for 30 minutes. Spread the Cilantro-Chile Pesto evenly over the cream cheese and chill. Beat the remaining cream cheese with the tomato salsa and spread it over the Cilantro-Chile Pesto. Chill for at least 4 hours.

► Just before serving, make the Avocado Salsa. (Or make the Avocado Salsa in advance and add the avocado at the last minute.) Place a serving dish on top of the dish containing the spread and, holding the 2 dishes tightly together, invert them both. Gently pull the plastic wrap so that the spread drops onto the serving dish, remove the top dish, and carefully peel off the plastic wrap. Spoon the Avocado Salsa over the top of the spread. Serve immediately.

St George's market in Grenada. Salsas are very much a part of the cuisine of the Caribbean.

Prosciutto Shrimp

Makes 4 servings

Prosciutto is Italian ham that has been cured in a spiced brine, then air-dried and aged for about a year. Because its flavor is so concentrated by this process, only a paper-thin slice is needed. In this simple but elegant appetizer, fruit and shrimp are wrapped in prosciutto and topped with Mango Salsa. If serving as a first course, allow 3 per person.

INGREDIENTS

12 medium to large shrimp, cooked and cleaned
2 tbsp fresh lime juice
3 fresh figs, quartered, or 12 small wedges of honeydew melon
6 large or 12 small slices of prosciutto
1 cup Mango Salsa (page 46)

METHOD

► Toss the shrimp with the lime juice. Let sit for 5 minutes, then drain off the juice if necessary.

► Pair each shrimp with a fig quarter or melon wedge. Cut large slices of prosciutto in half lengthwise. Wrap prosciutto around the fruit and shrimp. Top with Mango Salsa.

51

Hot Bean Dip

Makes about 2 cups

This easy recipe uses canned refried beans as a base, then adds spices, cheese, and Salsa Cruda to make it a flavorful dip. Serve it hot, with thick chips for dipping.

INGREDIENTS

1¹/₂ cups canned refried beans
1¹/₂ cups Salsa Cruda (pages 18–19)
1¹/₂ cups grated Cheddar or Jack cheese
¹/₄ tsp ground cumin
¹/₄ tsp dried oregano
salt if needed (depending on the saltiness of the beans)
¹/₄ cup sliced black olives
2 tbsp chopped green onions

METHOD

▶ Heat the beans in a pan until bubbly. Add the salsa, 1 cup cheese, the cumin and oregano. Stir until the cheese has melted, then taste and add salt if needed. Spoon into a heat-resistant serving dish and garnish with the remaining cheese, the olives and green onions.

Note: If desired, garnish first with cheese only. Put the bowl in a 350°F oven for a few minutes until the cheese is melted. Then garnish with the olives and green onions.

Chorizo-Bean Dip

Makes 2½ to 3 cups

Black beans puréed with spicy chorizo sausage and salsa make a delicious hot dip for chips. The leftovers are so good in omelets, empanadas (page 60), and tostaditas (page 63) that you'll want to make a double batch.

Ingredients

1 cup dried black beans
about 5 ounces chorizo sausage
½ cup chopped onion
1 to 2 tsp salt
1 cup Salsa Cruda I (page 18)

Method

▶ Sort through the beans and discard any pebbles or other debris. Soak the beans overnight in 4 cups water, or bring the beans and water to a boil, boil for 2 minutes, then turn off the heat and let sit, covered, for 1 hour. Drain and rinse the beans. Put the beans in a medium saucepan with 4 cups water. Bring to a boil, reduce the heat and simmer.

▶ Crumble the chorizo into a small skillet and fry until browned, 5 to 7 minutes. Tilt the pan to drain the grease, remove the meat with a slotted spoon and add to the beans. Discard all but 1 tbsp grease in the skillet. Reheat, and add the chopped onion. Sauté for 5 minutes, then add to the beans. Continue simmering the beans until tender, adding a little more water, if needed, so that there is still some cooking liquid left when the beans are done. The total cooking time should be 1 to 1½ hours. Stir in 1 tsp salt.

▶ Remove the pan from the heat and set aside about ⅓ cup beans. Purée the rest in a blender or food processor, then stir in the whole beans and the salsa. Taste and add more salt if necessary. Serve warm.

Chicken-Avocado Salsa Spread

Makes 1½ to 2 cups

This spread is more delicately flavored than most of the recipes in this book. If you want it to have more kick, add a chopped jalapeño, seeds and veins included, or some hot pepper sauce. You can make the spread in advance, but don't add the avocado until the last minute. Marinating and grilling the chicken, as on page 110, will give the spread additional flavor, but any method of cooking the chicken will do.

INGREDIENTS

¾ cup finely chopped cooked chicken
1 cup Grilled Salsa (page 26)
1 large avocado, peeled, pitted and mashed
1 tbsp lemon juice
salt to taste
cilantro leaves or chopped green onion for garnish (optional)

METHOD

▶ Combine all the ingredients and garnish with cilantro or green onion, if desired. Serve with crackers.

Nachos

54

Makes 3 to 4 servings

Homemade nachos are easy to make, and with real cheese and lots of extras they're better than most commercial versions. The joy of homemade nachos is that you can prepare them to suit your own taste. This deluxe version calls for tomatoes, avocados, olives, green onions, and salsa.

INGREDIENTS

10 to 12-ounce bag of tortilla chips
3 cups grated Cheddar or Jack cheese, or a combination
2 or 3 jalapeño chiles, fresh or canned, cut crosswise into thin slices
2 medium tomatoes, seeded and chopped
⅓ cup chopped green onions
2 to 3 ounces black olives, pitted and sliced
1 large ripe avocado, peeled, pitted, and diced, or Avocado Salsa (page 22) or Guacamole (page 17)
1 cup tomato-based salsa, such as Basic Cooked Salsa (page 32)

METHOD

▶ Preheat the oven to 400°F. Mound the chips on 1 or 2 oven-safe serving platters, layering with the cheese and jalapeños. Bake until the cheese is melted, 3 to 5 minutes. Remove from the oven and sprinkle with the tomatoes, green onions, olives and avocados. Serve with salsa on the side.

Layered Fiesta Dip

Makes about 10 to 12 servings

This hearty dip is made of layers of beans, sour cream, salsas, cheese and garnishes. I like to use a variety of salsas for a range of flavors – perhaps Roast Jalapeño Salsa (page 16) or Chipotle Salsa (page 34) with the beans, and a tomato-based salsa in the sour cream. Avoid salsas made with uncooked tomatoes, as the liquid from the tomatoes will pool in the sour cream. Serve with chips and raw vegetables.

INGREDIENTS

1¹/₂ cups refried beans
¹/₂ cup salsa of your choice
1 cup grated Jack cheese
1¹/₂ cups sour cream
¹/₂ cup second salsa of your choice
1¹/₂ cups Avocado Salsa (page 22)
1¹/₂ cups grated Cheddar cheese
¹/₂ cup chopped green onions
¹/₂ cup sliced black olives, well-drained
1 avocado, peeled, pitted and diced

METHOD

► Preheat the oven to 350°F. Mix the beans with the first salsa, spread this mixture on a large ovenproof platter, and sprinkle the Jack cheese evenly across the top. Put in the oven until the beans are hot and the cheese has melted, about 10 minutes.

► While the beans are heating, mix the sour cream with the second salsa. Remove the beans from the oven and spread the sour cream and salsa mixture on top, then the Avocado Salsa. Finally sprinkle the Cheddar cheese over the top. Garnish with the green onions, olives and avocado.

56

Sorting green chiles into bags for sale.

Seafood Salsa Spread

Makes 4 to 6 servings

This simple spread is made by combining salsa and seafood, then pouring it over a block of cream cheese. Use a tomato-based salsa of your choice, but it should be a cooked salsa or one made with grilled tomatoes, as raw tomatoes will exude watery juice. Serve with crackers or raw vegetables.

INGREDIENTS

1 cup tomato-based salsa
about 3 ounces tiny cooked shrimp or
  crabmeat
8-ounce block of cream cheese

METHOD

▶ Mix the salsa and shrimp or crabmeat. Place the cream cheese on a serving dish and pour the salsa over the top.

58

Homemade Tortilla Chips

Makes 4 to 6 servings

Sometimes, nothing but warm tortilla chips will do with homemade salsas. Fortunately they are not difficult to make. However, unless you have two large skillets, you'll be able to fry only a few chips at a time.

INGREDIENTS

12 stale tortillas
⅓ cup salt (optional)
oil for frying

METHOD

▶ To make the chips, cut stale tortillas into strips or wedges. (If the tortillas are fresh, dry them slightly by spreading them out and letting them sit for an hour or so.) If you want salted chips, make a brine of ⅓ cup salt and 2 cups of water. Briefly dip the tortilla pieces into the brine, then shake off the excess water.

▶ Pour ½ inch of vegetable oil into a large skillet and heat until the oil is hot but not smoking. Add the chips. If they are wet with brine, take care because the oil will splatter. Cook the chips until golden, turning once or twice, about 3 minutes, depending on how hot the oil is. Remove the chips from the oil, holding them briefly over the pan to drain off excess oil, then place them on paper towels to drain thoroughly. Give the oil a few moments to reheat, then add a new batch of chips.

▶ A fat-free cooking alternative is to bake the chips. Preheat the oven to 325°F. Spread the prepared tortillas in a single layer on an ungreased baking sheet. Bake, turning occasionally, until they are crisp and lightly browned, about 40 minutes.

Empanadas

Makes about 30

Empanadas are little Mexican meat pies, baked or fried. Traditional empanadas may have a crust made of masa harina, the ground corn used for making tortillas and tamales, while some modern interpretations use envelopes of phyllo dough. This recipe uses a pie crust dough to enclose a spicy-sweet meat filling flavored with salsa.

INGREDIENTS FOR THE CRUST

3 cups all-purpose flour
1½ tsp salt
1 cup plus 3 tbsp lard or solid shortening
6 tbsp cold water

METHOD

▶ Mix together the flour and salt, then cut in the fat with 2 sharp knives, a pastry cutter, or in a food processor, until the mixture resembles fine crumbs. Stir in the water. If using a food processor, do this step by hand so you can feel the moisture in the dough. The dough should form a moist ball. If it is too crumbly, add 1 tsp water at a time until it is moist but not sticky. Refrigerate for at least 1 hour, then remove and let it return to room temperature, approximately 1 hour, before rolling.

▶ Pinch off about half the dough. Roll out on a floured board to a thickness of ⅛ inch or less. Cut out 3-inch circles, then gather up the scraps, add to the rest of the dough, and roll out another batch. This should be enough dough for about 30 empanadas.

60

INGREDIENTS FOR THE SAVORY MEAT FILLING

1 pound lean ground beef
½ cup chopped onion
2 cups Salsa Cruda (pages 18–19), drained of excess liquid
⅓ cup toasted slivered almonds coarsely chopped (see Note 1 below)
⅓ cup raisins
½ tsp ground cumin
½ tsp ground cloves
1 tsp salt
¼ tsp pepper

METHOD

▶ Sauté the ground beef and onion in a hot skillet until the meat is browned, about 6 to 8 minutes. Add the salsa and cook for about 5 minutes to get rid of any excess liquid. Add the remaining ingredients, mix well and cook for 2 minutes longer.

▶ Place a spoonful of filling in the center of each circle of pastry. Fold over the pastry and seal the edges so it forms a crescent.

▶ Empanadas can be glazed (see Note 2 below) and baked until golden in a 400°F oven, about 15 minutes. Or they can be deep-fried in oil at 375°F until golden brown, 1 to 2 minutes a side. If you fry them, make sure the edges are well sealed so the filling doesn't leak out.

Note 1: To toast almonds, spread them in a single layer on a small baking sheet. Bake in a 350°F oven for 8 to 10 minutes, until golden brown.

Note 2: To make a glaze, with a fork lightly beat 2 eggs with ¼ cup milk or cream. Brush the glaze over the empanadas before baking.

Chile con Queso

Makes 4 to 6 servings

This hot cheese dip seasoned with roast chiles is popular in Texas and New Mexico. It is served bubbling hot from the oven with tortilla chips. Since it is a dense mixture, use thick chips, not thin ones that crumble easily. You can use leftover Roast Jalapeño Salsa (page 16), or make the simpler roast chile salsa below.

INGREDIENTS

2 cups grated Jack cheese, tightly packed
⅔ cup Roast Jalapeño Salsa (page 16)

METHOD

▶ Preheat the oven to 350°F. Mix the cheese and salsa in an ovenproof serving dish and bake until the cheese is bubbling, about 10 minutes. Serve immediately.

▶ As an alternative, make a simple salsa by roasting about 8 jalapeño chiles until the skins blister and turn brown. Put roast jalapeños in a bag for 10 minutes so steam will loosen the skins. Scrape the skins off the chiles, then remove the stems. Cut in half lengthwise and remove seeds and veins. Finely chop the jalapeños and mix with 1 minced clove garlic and 2 tbsp minced green onion.

62

Tostaditas

63

Tostaditas, or little tostadas, make great finger food. Start with round tortilla chips as a base and build individual appetizers. Use shredded beef or chicken, or refried beans, then add cheese, olives, avocados, salsa, green onions, sliced jalapeños, or any other toppings you like. Assemble them in advance for guests (but not too far in advance, since you don't want them to get soggy) or lay out the fixings and let them build their own. Below are some suggestions.

10- to 12-ounce bag tortilla chips

One or more of the following:
Chorizo-Bean Dip (page 53)
Shredded beef mixed with Red Chile Sauce
    (page 33)
cooked whole shrimp
shredded chicken

One or two kinds of cheese:
Something traditional like Cheddar or Jack,
    and a more unusual choice, such as goat
    cheese or Roquefort

Two kinds of salsa:
A traditional dipping salsa, and a less
    predictable choice, such as Chipotle Salsa
    (page 34) or Sweet Red Pepper Salsa
    (page 20)

Use a selection of the following garnishes:
One or two kinds of olives
Strips of roasted sweet red pepper or poblanos
Rings of fresh or pickled jalapeño chiles
Chopped green onions
Diced avocado
Sprigs of cilantro

▶ Layer the desired toppings on each chip and eat.

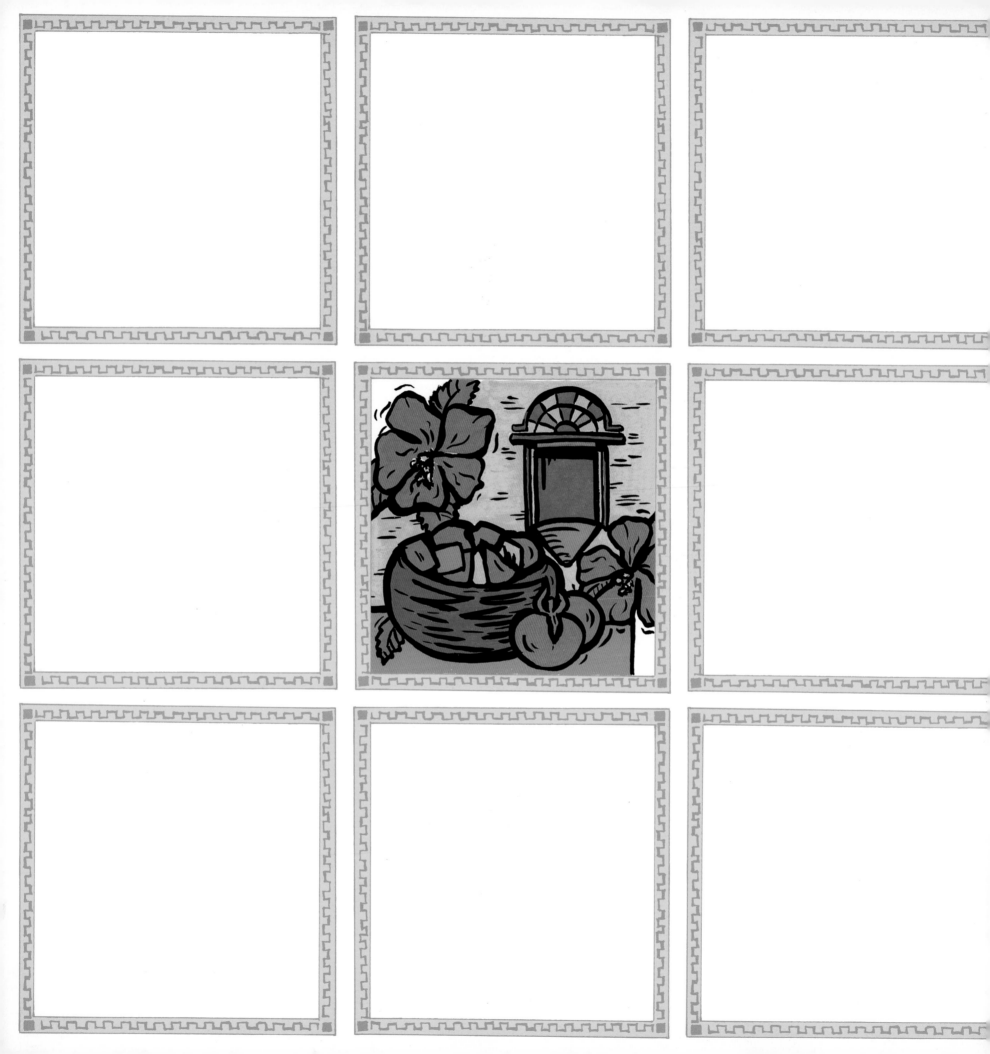

salads

Avocado-Shrimp Boats
Salmon Salad with Black
Bean-Papaya Salsa
Tomato Salad with Olive Salsa
Corn Salsa Salad with Avocados
Black-eyed Pea Salad
Fajita Salad
Jicama-Orange Salad
Chicken-Rice Salad

Avocado-Shrimp Boats

Makes 4 servings

In this salad, spicy fruit salsa is combined with the cool, mellow flavor of perfectly ripe avocado. It makes an excellent first course. Try fresh crab as a substitute for the tiny Bay shrimp. You can make the salsa and mix in the shrimp in advance, but don't cut the avocados until just before serving as they tend to brown quickly.

INGREDIENTS

4 ounces cooked Bay shrimp
1 cup Mango Salsa (page 46) or Nectarine Salsa (page 45)
2 ripe but firm avocados

METHOD

▶ Mix the shrimp with the salsa. Cut the avocados in half and scoop out the pits. Mound the salsa into the avocado halves. If absolutely necessary, scoop out a little of the avocado flesh to make room for the salsa.

66

Salmon Salad
with Black Bean-Papaya Salsa

Makes 4 servings

This simple salad is topped with an exotic salsa rather than salad dressing, for an exciting and unusual combination.

INGREDIENTS

6 cups mixed salad greens
12 to 16 ounces Grilled Salmon (page 122), chilled
2 cups Black Bean-Papaya Salsa (page 46)

METHOD

▶ Clean and tear the salad greens and divide them among 4 plates. Break the salmon into chunks, removing any bones. Divide the salmon among the plates. Top each salad with ½ cup Black Bean-Papaya Salsa.

Tomato Salad with Olive Salsa

Makes 4 servings

This simple salad depends on excellent ingredients – perfectly ripe tomatoes, fresh (not packaged) mozzarella cheese, and fresh basil leaves. Top it with Olive Salsa for a luscious summer dish.

Ingredients

4 large, ripe tomatoes
several stems of fresh basil
4 ounces fresh mozzarella cheese
about 1 cup Olive Salsa (page 22)

Method

► Core the tomatoes and cut them into thick slices. Arrange the slices on 4 salad plates. Rinse the basil, pull off the leaves and dry them between paper towels. Arrange the basil leaves on top of the tomato slices. Cut the mozzarella into thin slices and place on top of the tomato and basil. Spoon the olive salsa over the tomatoes and cheese.

68

Tomatoes for sale in a market in Mexico.

Corn Salsa Salad with Avocados

Makes 8 servings

This pretty, crunchy salad is an excellent dish for a picnic or barbecue. It can be made early in the day except for the avocados, which should be added at the last minute.

INGREDIENTS

4 cups Corn Salsa (page 21)
1 cup cooked corn
15-ounce can of kidney beans, rinsed and drained
1 small, thin zucchini, thinly sliced
3 cloves garlic, minced
2 tbsp chopped fresh cilantro
¼ tsp ground cumin
2 ripe avocados, peeled, pitted and cubed

METHOD

▶ Mix the Corn Salsa with the corn, kidney beans, zucchini, garlic, cilantro, and cumin. Add the avocado just before serving, and stir in well so it is thoroughly coated with the salsa. Taste and adjust the seasoning.

Black-eyed Pea Salad

Makes 8 servings

This zesty side dish is well suited to a picnic or barbecue. It is best when very spicy, so be sure to make the salsa with jalapeño seeds, or add an extra jalapeño with seeds. The black-eyed peas have a pleasantly nutty flavor, but you can substitute other beans, such as white beans. This recipe calls for canned beans, but if you have time to soak and cook dried beans, it will improve the flavor. Make the salad several hours in advance, but no more than 12 hours or it will start to lose its crunchy texture.

INGREDIENTS

3 1-pound cans of cooked black-eyed peas, rinsed and drained
3 to 3½ cups Salsa Cruda III (page 19), made with an additional jalapeño if desired
2 tbsp red wine vinegar
2 tbsp olive oil
salt and pepper to taste

METHOD

▶ Combine all the ingredients. Refrigerate for at least 2 hours before serving.

71

Fajita Salad

Makes 4 servings

Crisp lettuce is topped with fajita meat, avocado, and raw vegetables, then served with a spicy salsa instead of a traditional dressing. It is a great way to use leftovers from a fajita party. Use Grilled Chicken (page 110), Salsa-marinated Flank Steak (page 109), or beef grilled for Fajitas (page 98).

INGREDIENTS

6 cups romaine or other lettuce
12 ounces cold grilled meat, cut into thin
strips
1 avocado, peeled, pitted and diced
several thin slices of red onion, separated
into rings
several radishes, thinly sliced
1 small bell pepper, cut into strips
1 to 1¹/₂ cups tomato-based salsa

METHOD

▶ Divide the lettuce among 4 large plates. Top with the meat, avocado, onion, radishes and bell pepper. Serve the salsa on the side.

Jicama-Orange Salad

Makes 4 to 6 servings

This refreshing salad combines the crunch of fresh jicama, the tang of oranges, the bite of onion and the heat of jalapeño chile. It is served with a slightly sweet dressing for an unusual flavor.

INGREDIENTS

3 medium oranges
¹/₂ medium red onion
1 cup peeled jicama, cut into ¹/₂-inch cubes
dressing (recipe follows)
lettuce leaves

METHOD

▶ Peel the oranges and slice them thinly, removing the seeds. Thinly slice the onion, then separate the slices into rings. Mix the orange, onion and jicama together, toss with the dressing, and serve over lettuce.

DRESSING

¹/₂ cup olive oil
¹/₄ cup red wine vinegar
2 tbsp orange juice
2 tsp honey
¹/₄ tsp chili powder
1 jalapeño chile, unseeded, finely chopped

METHOD

▶ Combine all the ingredients in a bottle and shake well to mix.

Chicken-Rice Salad

Makes 4 to 6 servings

Serve this salad on a bed of lettuce for a delicious luncheon dish. It is best when the chicken is marinated and grilled, as for Grilled Chicken (page 110), but any cooked chicken will do.

INGREDIENTS

3 cups cooked white rice
2 chicken breast halves, cooked and cubed
1¹/₂ cups Salsa Cruda III (page 19)
¹/₄ cup chopped green onions
¹/₃ cup toasted slivered almonds (see right)
1 avocado, peeled, pitted and diced
1 tbsp red wine vinegar
salt to taste

METHOD

▶ Combine all the ingredients. Taste and adjust the seasonings.

To toast almonds: Spread them in a single layer on a small baking sheet. Bake at 350°F until golden brown, 7 to 10 minutes.

7 3

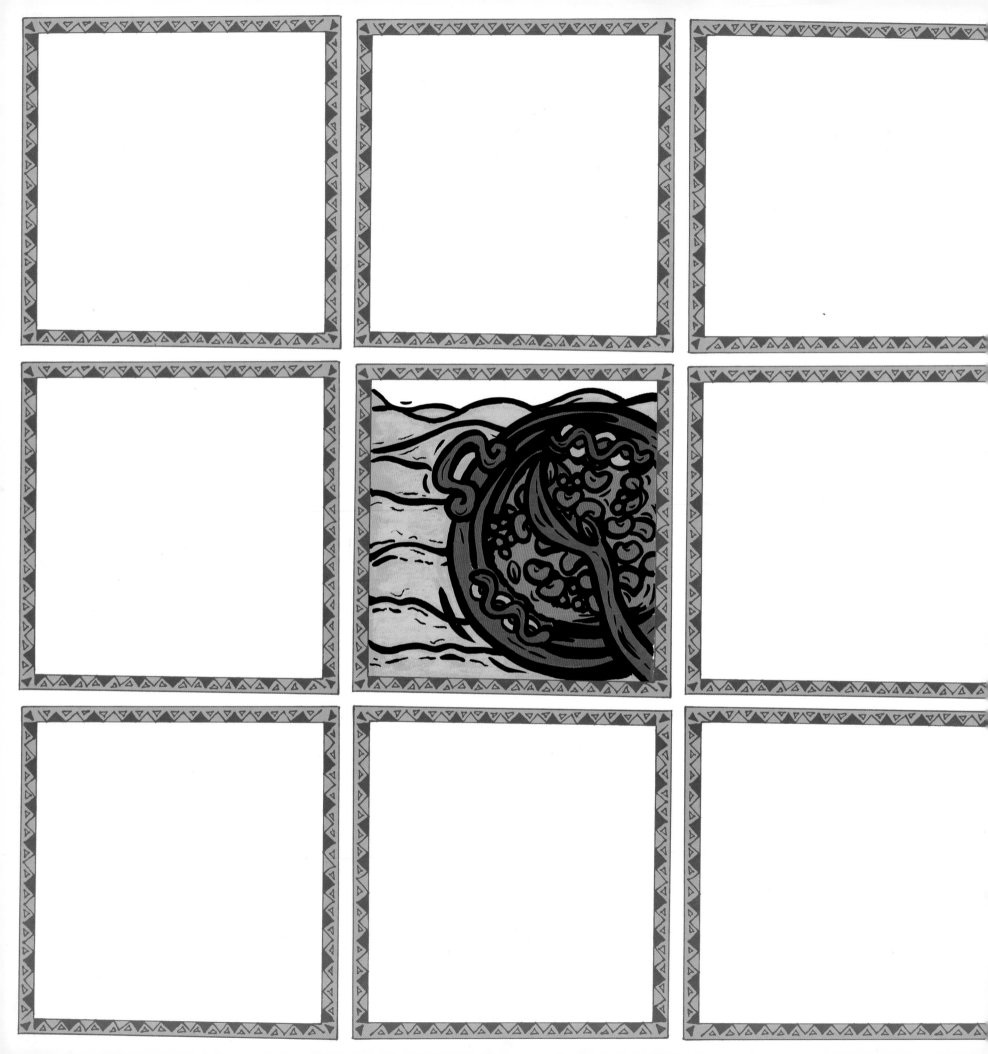

soups, stews and bean dishes

Avocado Soup
Tomato-Basil Soup with
Sweet Red Pepper Salsa
Lime-Tortilla Soup
Spicy Crab-Corn Chowder
Black Bean Soup with Chorizo
Pozole

Grilled Seafood Soup
Red Beans and Rice
Feijoada

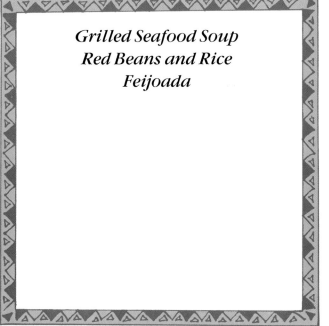

Avocado Soup

76

Makes 4 servings

This easy, no-cook soup is wonderful on a summer day, when avocados are plentiful and cheap. Be sure that the avocados are perfectly ripe, but not overripe, since this soup showcases their flavor. Serve it cold, garnished with a crunchy salsa. Although the soup needs to be made at least 2 hours in advance, it does not keep well if made more than 8 hours in advance.

INGREDIENTS

3 ripe avocados, peeled and pitted
1¼ cups chicken broth
1 cup light cream
1 tsp salt
¼ tsp cayenne
1 cup Cucumber Salsa (page 20) or Salsa Cruda III (page 19)

METHOD

▶ Put all the ingredients except the salsa in a blender or food processor and purée until smooth. Chill for at least 2 hours. Stir well to blend in any darkening on the surface and serve, garnished with the salsa.

Tomato-Basil Soup
with Sweet Red Pepper Salsa

Makes 4 servings

This is a delightful hot-weather soup, perfect for late summer when the garden is producing an abundance of tomatoes. Don't use hard, pink, grocery-store tomatoes, since this recipe relies on the lush flavor of ripe tomatoes. The soup should be made early in the day, then chilled until serving time. For a slightly spicier flavor, substitute Roast Jalapeño Salsa (page 16) for the Sweet Red Pepper Salsa.

INGREDIENTS

2 cloves garlic, minced
5 tbsp chopped fresh basil
¼ tsp freshly ground black pepper
3 tbsp extra-virgin olive oil
4 pounds ripe tomatoes

1 cup chicken broth
1 tbsp balsamic vinegar
½ tsp salt
about ½ cup Sweet Red Pepper Salsa
(page 20)

METHOD

▶ In a small bowl, mix together the garlic, 1 tbsp basil, the black pepper and olive oil. Lightly crush the garlic with the back of a spoon to release the juices into the oil. Let the mixture steep while you prepare the tomatoes.

▶ Peel the tomatoes by dropping them into a pot of boiling water for about 40 seconds. Let

them cool slightly, then slip off the skins. Cut them in half and squeeze out the seeds. Core and coarsely chop the tomatoes.

▶ Put the tomatoes, chicken broth, and garlic-oil mixture into a medium saucepan. Bring to a boil, then reduce the heat to low and simmer, uncovered, for 1 hour. Add the remaining basil, the balsamic vinegar and salt, then purée the soup. Taste and adjust the seasonings. Chill until serving time.

▶ Top each bowl of soup with 1 to 2 tablespoons Sweet Red Pepper Salsa, which should be stirred into the soup.

Lime-Tortilla Soup

Makes 4 main-course servings

This is a variation on a traditional Mexican soup – chicken broth flavored with salsa and lime, poured over tortilla chips and shredded chicken, then garnished with cheese. Make sure you include some jalapeño seeds when you make the salsa, or the soup will be only mildly spicy. Ideally the chicken should be marinated in lime juice, olive oil and garlic, then grilled, but boiled, poached or roast chicken are fine too. You can use packaged tortilla chips, but it's even better when you make your own by frying strips of tortilla in hot oil.

INGREDIENTS

1 1/2 cups Salsa Cruda I (page 18)
4 cups chicken broth
2 tortillas
2 to 3 tbsp vegetable oil
2 chicken breast halves, cooked and shredded
2 tbsp fresh lime juice
salt to taste
grated Jack cheese or dry Mexican cheese, for garnish

METHOD

► Cut the tortillas into chip-size strips. Heat the oil in a skillet until it is very hot but not smoking. Quickly fry the tortilla strips in batches until they are crisp, 1 to 2 minutes a side. Drain on paper towels.

► Put the salsa and chicken broth in a large saucepan. Bring to a boil, reduce the heat and simmer, covered, for 15 minutes. Meanwhile, divide the tortilla chips and shredded chicken among 4 soup bowls.

► In a blender or food processor, purée the soup in batches. Return the soup to the stove and add the lime and salt to taste. Simmer for about 2 minutes longer for flavors to blend. Pour into the soup bowls, sprinkle cheese on top, and serve immediately.

78

Spicy Crab-Corn Chowder

Makes 6 servings

In this delicious crab soup, Roast Corn Salsa is cooked with chicken broth, cream and crabmeat for a smoky, chunky, slightly spicy cream soup. You will fall instantly in love with it. Use fresh crab rather than canned – you'll be able to taste the difference. If you prefer a spicier soup, leave some of the seeds in the jalapeño when you make the salsa, or add another jalapeño and seeds to the soup.

INGREDIENTS

2 tbsp butter
1/2 cup chopped onion
3 cups chicken broth
3 cups Roast Corn Salsa (page 29)
1 cup heavy cream
1/2 tsp salt
1/4 tsp white pepper
1 cup sour cream
1/2 pound fresh cooked crabmeat
1 tbsp chopped fresh cilantro
2 green onions, chopped

METHOD

► Melt the butter in a large, heavy saucepan. Sauté the onion for 5 minutes or until tender. Add the chicken broth and Roast Corn Salsa. Bring the soup to a boil, then lower the heat, place a cover on the pot slightly askew, and simmer for 20 minutes.

► Add the heavy cream, salt and white pepper, and return to a boil, then whisk in the sour cream and crabmeat. Heat just a couple minutes to warm the sour cream and crab, but don't bring it to a boil as it may curdle. Ladle the soup into bowls and garnish with the cilantro and green onion.

Black Bean Soup with Chorizo

80

Makes 6 servings

This soup is full of flavor even before you top it with salsa. Some of the spiciness comes from the chorizo sausage, but since chorizo can vary widely, you will need to taste the soup and adjust the seasoning to taste, adding some ground cumin if necessary. Purée the soup if you prefer it smooth.

INGREDIENTS

2 cups dried black beans
6 cups chicken broth
2 large tomatoes, seeded and chopped
1 tbsp red wine vinegar
2 ancho chiles
1 pound chorizo sausage
1½ cups chopped onion
2 stalks celery, diced
3 cloves garlic, minced
2 to 3 tsp salt
½ tsp pepper
½ to 2 tsp ground cumin (optional)
1 to 1½ cups Salsa Cruda I or III (pages 18–19)
sour cream (optional), for garnish

METHOD

► Pick over the beans, removing any pebbles, then put them in a large saucepan with 6 cups water. Bring to a boil, boil for 2 minutes, then cover and turn off the heat. Let sit for 1 hour. Drain and rinse the beans, and put them back in the pot with the chicken broth, 3 cups of water, the chopped tomatoes and the vinegar. Bring to a boil, reduce the heat, and simmer, uncovered, until the beans are tender and the excess liquid has been absorbed, about 1 to 1½ hours.

► Meanwhile, prepare the ancho chiles. Cut them in half, remove the stems and some of the seeds. Put them in a small, heat-resistant bowl. Pour ½ cup boiling water over the anchos and let them steep for 30 minutes, stirring once or twice to be sure all of them are soaking. Drain and discard the water. Put the anchos and ½ cup of fresh water into a blender or food processor and purée. Add the purée to the beans.

► Next, prepare the chorizo and vegetables. Remove the sausage skin and crumble the meat into a skillet. Fry until the excess fat has cooked out. Tilt the pan to drain the sausage, remove the sausage with a slotted spoon and add to the beans.

► Discard all but 1 tbsp of chorizo fat. Add the onion and celery to the fat and sauté for 5 minutes. Add the garlic and sauté for 1 minute longer. Add the vegetables to the beans.

► When the beans are tender, taste and add salt, pepper, and cumin if needed. Simmer for 2 minutes longer to allow the flavors to blend. If desired, purée the soup in batches. (The soup can be made in advance to this point and refrigerated.) Return the soup to the pan and briefly reheat it. Ladle into soup bowls and garnish with salsa and with sour cream, if desired.

Pozole

Makes 8 main-course servings

Pozole, a long-simmering pork and hominy stew, is a traditional dish that dates back many centuries with Mexicans and American Indians of the Southwest. Historically, it is made with dried hominy and the broth is often cooked with pigs' feet. However, dried hominy is not readily available in many communities, and some people are squeamish about using pigs' feet. For those reasons, and as a shortcut, this recipe uses canned hominy and neck bones instead. Other pork bones may be used too. This version of pozole is a main dish, but you can omit the cubed pork and serve it as a side dish or first course, if you prefer. Serve with Cucumber Salsa or Salsa Cruda II, to be spooned over the stew.

INGREDIENTS

¾ cup chopped onion
4 tbsp vegetable oil
3 cloves garlic, minced
2 quarts chicken broth
1 pound pork neck bones
2 ancho chiles
2 dried California chiles
3 tbsp flour
1 tsp salt

1 tsp dried mustard
2 tsp dried oregano
2 tsp ground cumin
½ tsp cayenne
½ tsp black pepper
3 pounds pork roast or other pork cut, cut into bite-sized cubes
4 cups canned hominy
2 to 3 cups Cucumber Salsa (page 20) or Salsa Cruda III (page 18)

METHOD

▶ In a large stockpot, sauté the onion in 1 tbsp oil for 5 minutes. Add the garlic and cook for 1 minute longer, then add the chicken broth and neck bones. Note the level of the liquid, then add 2 cups water. If the broth falls below that level during cooking, add more water. Bring the stew to a boil, reduce the heat, and simmer, uncovered, for 2 hours.

▶ While the stew is simmering, cut the dried chiles in half and remove the seeds. Put the chiles in a small, heat-resistant bowl and pour ½ cup boiling water over them. Let soak for 20 minutes, stirring once or twice to be sure all parts of chiles are softened. Purée the water and chiles in a blender, then add this purée to the simmering stew.

▶ After the stew has simmered for 2 hours, remove it from the heat. Remove the pork bones. If you have time, let the broth and the bones cool for ease of handling. Skim the fat from the broth and return the broth to the stove. Take off any meat from the bones and add it to the stew. Discard the bones and fat.

▶ Mix together the flour, salt, mustard, oregano, cumin, cayenne and black pepper. Toss the pork cubes in this seasoning mixture until evenly coated. Heat the remaining oil in a large skillet and sauté the pork just until it is golden brown. Add the pork cubes to the stew, bring to a boil, then reduce the heat and simmer, covered, for 20 minutes. Add the hominy and simmer for 10 minutes longer.

▶ Taste the broth and adjust the salt to taste. Ladle the pozole into large bowls and serve with Cucumber Salsa or Salsa Cruda III on the side.

81

Ocotlán market in Mexico.

Grilled Seafood Soup

Makes 4 servings

The flavors of grilled seafood and salsa combine for a spicy soup that is low in fat. This recipe calls for shrimp and scallops, but you can substitute other grilled seafood or fish. The size is not important (tiny Bay shrimp are not recommended), although smaller pieces may fall through the grill. You can also substitute a different salsa – any smooth, tomato-based one is good. Since the spiciness of the soup depends on the salsa, a fairly hot one is recommended.

INGREDIENTS

3/4 pound shrimp, peeled and deveined
3/4 pound scallops
1/4 cup olive oil
1/4 cup fresh lime juice
3 cloves garlic, minced
1 tbsp vegetable oil
2 to 2 1/2 cups Basic Cooked Salsa (page 32)

5 cups clam juice or seafood broth
1 tbsp fresh basil or 1 tsp dried
1 tsp fresh thyme or 1/4 tsp dried
3 thick slices of onion, separated into rings
1/2 bell pepper, cut into chunks
1 or 2 jalapeño chiles, thinly sliced into rounds
salt and pepper to taste

METHOD

► Put the seafood in a non-metallic bowl. Mix the olive oil, lime juice and garlic together, pour over the seafood, and stir so all the pieces are coated. Refrigerate the seafood while you prepare the barbecue. It will be easier to grill the seafood if it is threaded on skewers (wooden skewers should be soaked in water for 30 minutes to prevent burning) or if you use a special tray for grilling small items.

► Mound coals in the barbecue and let burn until the flames have died and the coals are glowing, 30 to 40 minutes. Spread the coals out. Put the seafood on the oiled grill or tray and cook for 2 to 3 minutes a side. It does not have to be thoroughly cooked since it can finish cooking in the soup, but it should pick up color and flavor from the grilling. If the pieces are large, cut into bite-sized chunks.

► Heat the vegetable oil in a large saucepan. Add the salsa and fry it for 5 minutes. Add the clam juice or seafood broth and the herbs. Bring to a boil, reduce the heat and simmer, with the lid slightly askew, for 15 minutes. Remove the cover and add the onion, bell pepper and jalapeño. Simmer for 3 to 4 minutes longer. Add the seafood and cook for 1 to 2 minutes. Add salt and pepper to taste.

82

A selection of fresh fish.

Red Beans and Rice

Makes 6 to 8 servings

From Central America to the Caribbean to New Orleans, slow-cooked and highly seasoned red beans and rice is a traditional dish. This main-course version uses leftover pork, but it's good with chunks of sausage or shreds of barbecued beef brisket too. Top with uncooked salsa for color, crunch and flavor.

INGREDIENTS

2 cups dried kidney beans
2 to 3 tbsp vegetable oil
1 cup chopped onion
2 stalks celery, chopped
3 cloves garlic, minced
2 cups cooked pork (diced ham, slivers of ham hocks, shredded barbecued or roast pork)
2 bay leaves
1 tsp ground cumin
½ tsp pepper
1 to 2 tsp salt
4 to 5 cups cooked rice
2 cups Salsa Cruda I (page 18) or Salsa Cruda III (page 19)
sour cream (optional)

METHOD

▶ Pick through the beans for pebbles or other debris. Put the beans in a large saucepan, add 6 cups water and soak overnight. Or you can bring the beans and water to a boil, boil for 2 minutes, then cover, turn off the heat, and let the beans sit for an hour.

▶ Drain and rinse the beans and put them back in the pot. Add enough water to cover the beans by about 2 inches, then bring to a boil. Meanwhile prepare the vegetables. Heat the oil in a skillet. Add the onion and celery and cook for 5 minutes, then add the garlic and cook for 2 minutes longer. Add the vegetables to the beans, along with the pork, bay leaves, cumin and pepper. Reduce the heat and simmer until the beans are tender, 1 to 1½ hours. Check periodically and add more water if needed. Taste and add salt.

▶ Serve the beans over rice, topped with the salsa and with sour cream if desired.

84

Feijoada

Makes 6 to 8 servings

Feijoada is a Brazilian stew of pork and black beans, traditionally eaten with rice and greens. This version uses Garlic Salsa for a wonderful garlicky flavor. Linguica, a hot Portuguese sausage, gives it its kick.

INGREDIENTS

2 cups dried black beans
1 pound pork loin, cut into ¾-inch cubes
salt and pepper to taste
2 cups Garlic Salsa (page 35)
2 tbsp fresh lemon juice
4 tbsp olive oil
1 pound linguica sausage, cut into ½-inch slices

METHOD

► Pick through the beans for pebbles or other debris. Put the beans in a large saucepan with 8 cups water. Let soak overnight, or bring the water to a boil, boil for 2 minutes, then remove from the heat, cover, and let soak for 1 hour.

► Put the pork in a non-metallic bowl and sprinkle with salt and pepper. Combine half the Garlic Salsa with the lemon juice and 2 tbsp olive oil, mix with the pork, and let it marinate for about 30 minutes. Drain the salsa, but do not discard. Heat the remaining oil in a large skillet and add the pork. Cook until the cubes are lightly browned, 6 to 8 minutes. They do not have to be cooked thoroughly.

► Drain and rinse the beans. Put them in a large stewpot and add enough water to cover the beans by 1 inch. Bring to a boil, then reduce the heat and simmer, uncovered. Check the beans occasionally and add a little more water if needed.

► Add the pork, the salsa that was used for marinade, and the remaining salsa to the beans, together with the linguica. Cook until the beans are tender, and the liquid has reduced to a thick sauce, 1 to 1½ hours. Taste and add more salt if necessary. Ladle into bowls and serve.

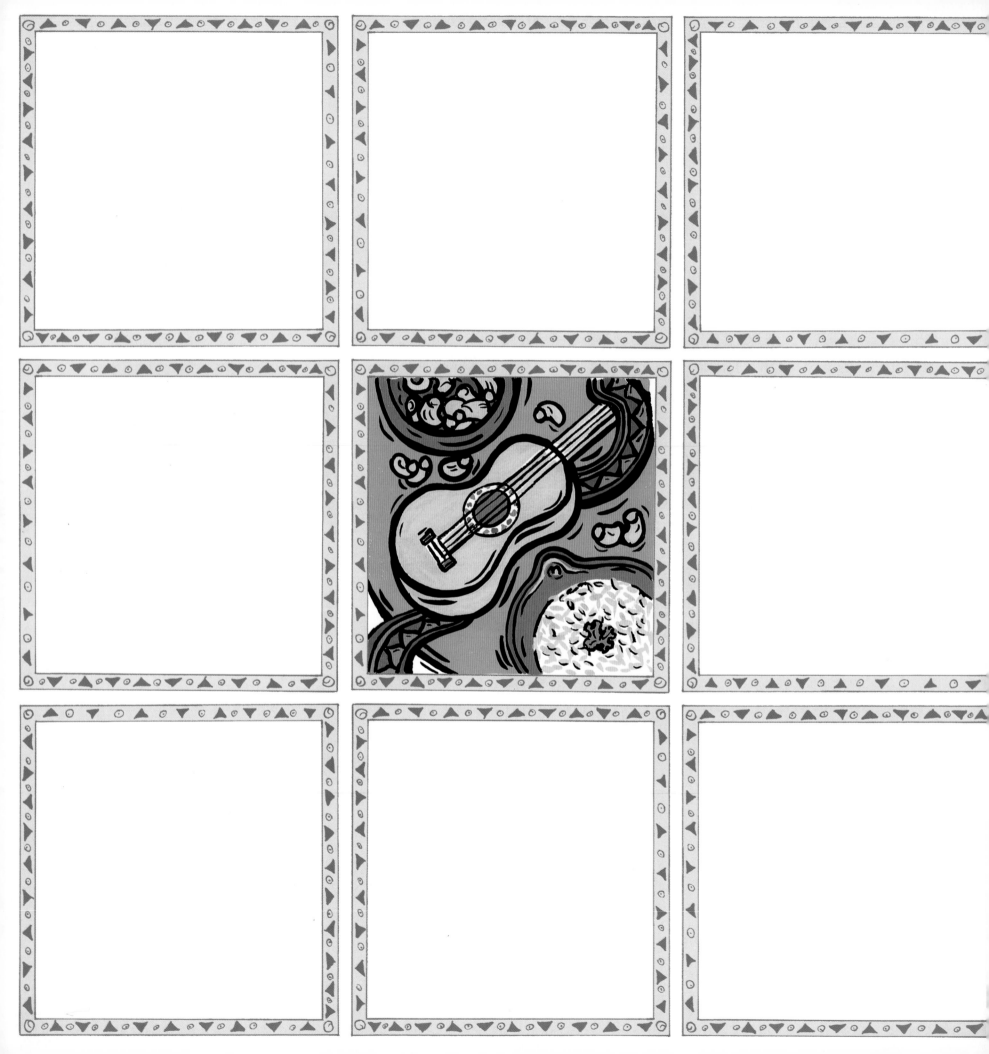

rice, pasta and side dishes

Pasta with Sun-dried Tomato Salsa
Corn Salsa Muffins
Spanish Rice
Fettucine with Shrimp and
Chile-Cream Sauce
Green Rice

Pasta with Sun-dried Tomato Salsa

88

Makes 4 first-course servings

**The intense flavors of this powerful salsa may
clash in concentrated form. When it is tossed
with pasta, however, the flavors meld and
become complementary.**

Ingredients

3 tbsp olive oil
6 cloves garlic, minced
1 tsp crushed dried chiles
*1 sweet red pepper, cored, seeded and cut into
    quarters*
4 ounces sun-dried tomatoes, packed in oil
1 tbsp chopped fresh basil
4 slices bacon, cooked and crumbled
2 ounces (about ¼ cup) sliced black olives
12 to 16 ounces pasta
grated Parmesan cheese

Method

▶ Heat the oil in a small skillet over low heat.
Add the minced garlic and the dried chiles.
Cook slowly, stirring often and pressing the
garlic to release the juices, until the garlic is
lightly browned, 5 to 8 minutes. The heat must
be very low or the garlic may scorch and turn
bitter. Remove from the heat and let steep
while you prepare the other ingredients.

▶ Grill the red pepper skin side down over a
barbecue fire or skin side up under a broiler
until the skin is blackened. Remove from the
heat and place it in a plastic bag to steam for
10 minutes. Peel off the skin and chop the red
pepper.

▶ Chop the sun-dried tomatoes and put them
into a small bowl with the basil. Add the
bacon, garlic-chile-olive oil mixture, red
pepper, and sliced olives. Cook the pasta in
plenty of boiling salted water until just tender.
Drain well, and then toss with the salsa and
Parmesan cheese.

Corn Salsa Muffins

Makes 12 to 18 muffins

These muffins are made spicy by the addition of Corn Salsa. Serve them with salads, soups, stews and chiles. The recipe makes 12 large muffins, or about 18 muffins if you fill the cups about ⅔ with batter.

INGREDIENTS

1½ cups cornmeal
½ cup all-purpose flour
1 tsp salt
2 tsp baking powder
1 tsp baking soda
1 tbsp sugar

3 eggs, lightly beaten
⅓ cup butter, melted
about 1 cup + 2 tbsp buttermilk
2 cups Corn Salsa (page 21)

METHOD

▶ Preheat the oven to 425°F. Lightly grease some muffin pans.

▶ Mix together all the dry ingredients in a large bowl. In a small bowl, mix the eggs, melted butter and 1 cup buttermilk. Pour the liquids into the dry ingredients and stir until combined. The batter may be a little lumpy as long as there aren't clumps of dry cornmeal. Stir in the salsa and add more buttermilk if needed. The batter should be fairly thick, so that it pours slowly. For large muffins, fill the cups to the rim. For smaller muffins, fill them two thirds full.

▶ Bake until the tops are lightly browned and a knife inserted in the center of a muffin comes out clean, about 18 to 24 minutes, depending on size.

Spanish Rice

Makes 6 to 8 servings

This is a spicier version of Spanish Rice than is usually served with Mexican food. The spices are briefly fried to develop their flavor, then rice is added and fried. It is then steamed in water and salsa.

INGREDIENTS

3 tbsp vegetable oil
1 tsp chili powder
1/2 tsp ground cumin
1/2 tsp dried oregano
2 cloves garlic, minced
2 cups white rice
1 1/2 cups Salsa Cruda I (page 18) or Salsa Cruda III (page 19)
1 tsp salt

90

METHOD

▶ Heat the oil in a heavy skillet. Add the chili powder, cumin, oregano and garlic and cook for 1 minute, stirring constantly. If the oil is very hot, remove the skillet from the heat and let the spices cook in the heat from the oil. After 1 minute, add the rice. Cook for 10 minutes, stirring almost constantly.

▶ If the skillet is large and deep (at least 7-cup capacity), add 2¾ cups water, the salsa and the salt. If the skillet is not large enough, transfer the seasoned rice to a large saucepan and add the water, salsa and salt. Bring to a boil, cover and reduce the heat. Cook until the liquid has been absorbed and the rice is tender, 20 to 25 minutes. Fluff with a fork. Let sit, covered, for another 5 minutes, then serve.

Olvera in the province of Cadiz.

Fettucine with Shrimp and Chile-Cream Sauce

Makes 6 first-course or 4 main-course servings

Here's a spicy variation on Fettucine Alfredo, with Roast Jalapeño Salsa and shrimp cooked in the cream sauce. Time this dish so that the fettucine finishes cooking just as the sauce is done. If it finishes a minute or two ahead of the sauce, toss with a scant amount of olive oil.

INGREDIENTS

6 tbsp butter
½ cup Roast Jalapeño Salsa (page 16)
¾ pound medium to large shrimp, cleaned
1 pound fettucine

1 cup heavy cream
½ tsp salt
pinch of white pepper
½ cup grated Parmesan cheese, plus additional for garnish

METHOD

▶ Melt 2 tbsp butter in a large skillet. Add 1 tbsp Roast Jalapeño Salsa and cook for 1 minute, stirring. Add the shrimp and sauté until they curl tightly and are an opaque white-pink, 2 to 3 minutes. Remove the shrimp with a slotted spoon and set aside.

▶ Cook the fettucine in plenty of boiling salted water until just tender, then drain. While the pasta is cooking, add the remaining butter to the skillet in which you cooked the shrimp. When it is melted and foamy, add the remaining salsa. Cook, stirring, for 1 minute, then add the cream, salt and white pepper, and cook until the sauce thickens slightly, about 3 minutes. Stir in the shrimp, then stir in the Parmesan cheese and the cooked, drained noodles. Toss until the noodles are coated. Serve with additional Parmesan sprinkled on top.

Green Rice

Makes 6 to 8 servings

This spicy rice dish is flavored with cilantro and Roast Jalapeño Salsa.

INGREDIENTS

1 cup Roast Jalapeño Salsa (page 16)
½ cup fresh cilantro
½ cup fresh parsley
3½ cups chicken broth
¼ cup vegetable oil
2 cups white rice
1½ tsp salt

METHOD

▶ In a blender or food processor, purée the salsa, cilantro and parsley with about 1 cup chicken broth. Set aside.

▶ Heat the oil in a skillet. Add the rice and cook, stirring frequently, 10 minutes. If the skillet does not have at least a 7-cup capacity, transfer the rice to a large saucepan. Add the purée, the remaining chicken broth and the salt to the rice. Bring to a boil, cover and reduce the heat. Cook until the liquid has been absorbed and the rice is tender, 20 to 25 minutes. Fluff the rice with a fork and let sit, covered, for another 5 minutes before serving.

mexican dishes

Quesadillas
Fajitas
Chicken Enchiladas with
Green Chile Sauce
Beef Enchiladas with
Red Chile Sauce
Tostadas
Black Bean Chiles Rellenos

Quesadillas

Quesadillas have become ubiquitous, showing up in all kinds of restaurants, Mexican or not, with a variety of fillings – goat cheese, smoked chicken, lobster, and just about anything else imaginable. True Mexican quesadillas are cheese empanadas – turnovers made with fresh corn tortilla masa. But here we go the easy route, using the flour tortilla version popular in the US.

Quesadillas are typically served with a tomato salsa, but don't overlook the possibilities of a tomatillo salsa, black bean salsa or avocado salsa. Or use two salsas – one type in the filling, and another for dipping. If you're feeling really bold, try a fruit salsa with a meat or fish filling.

The easiest way to cook quesadillas is over a griddle. But since many homes don't have a griddle, here are instructions for making them in a skillet.

96

INGREDIENTS

For each quesadilla, you will need:
vegetable oil or lard
1 flour tortilla
⅓ cup grated cheese or 2 4-inch squares of sliced Cheddar, Jack, or Mexican string cheese – or any type of cheese you prefer

METHOD

▶ Very lightly oil a heavy skillet that is at least as large as the tortilla (usually about 8 inches in diameter). You only need enough oil to season the tortilla and keep it from sticking. Heat the skillet, then place the tortilla in it, making sure it lies flat. Reduce the heat to low. Place the cheese on one half of the tortilla, and fold the other half over the cheese. Lightly brush the top of the folded tortilla with oil. As the cheese begins to melt and the quesadilla holds together, carefully turn it over. Cook until the cheese has completely melted and the tortilla has a few brown spots.

▶ Remove from the heat, cut into wedges, and serve with salsa for dipping.

▶ Instead of folding the tortilla, you can double the amount of cheese and make a sandwich with a second tortilla. This method is faster if you're cooking quesadillas for a large number of people.

▶ For variety, add any combination of the following to the cheese filling:

strips of roast poblano or jalapeño chiles, or sweet red pepper
chopped green onions
chopped cilantro
mushrooms sautéed in butter and garlic
cooked meat, such as grilled chicken, smoked sausage, beef or pork
cooked seafood, such as shrimp or crab
Black Bean Salsa (page 26)

▶ The following items are best cold, rather than cooked in the quesadilla, so serve them over the top, or pry open the cooked quesadilla and put them inside:

black olives
sliced avocado
chopped fresh tomatoes
sour cream (on top or as a dip)

Produce under protective awnings in a Mexican market.

Fajitas

98

Makes 4 servings

Fajitas, thinly-sliced grilled beef wrapped in tortillas and maybe salsa, sprang up in Texas in the 1970s, then swept the country in the 1980s. The original fajitas used a skirt steak off the diaphragm area of the steer, but many other cuts of beef are commonly used as well. From its simple beginnings, the fajita has become a garnish-laden meal, accompanied by cheese, guacamole and sour cream. This version keeps it simple: marinated grilled beef, salsa, and some sautéed peppers and onions are wrapped in flour tortillas. For variety, substitute Grilled Chicken (page 110) or grilled pork. Another marinade option is the one used in Salsa-marinated Flank Steak (page 109).

INGREDIENTS

1½ pounds skirt or flank steak
1½ cups beer
⅔ cup olive oil
¼ cup red wine vinegar
4 cloves garlic, minced
½ tsp salt
¼ tsp pepper
2 green bell peppers
1 medium onion
2 tbsp vegetable oil
12 flour tortillas
1 to 1½ cups salsa of your choice

METHOD

▶ Pierce the beef all over with a fork, then put it in a shallow glass dish. Make a marinade by combining the beer, olive oil, vinegar, garlic, salt and pepper. Pour the marinade over the beef, turning the meat to be sure it is completely coated. Marinate overnight.

▶ About an hour before you plan to eat, light a fire in the barbecue. Cut the bell peppers into strips. Cut the onion into thick horizontal slices, then separate the rings. Heat the oil in a skillet, and cook the onion slowly over low heat until golden, about 25 minutes. Add the pepper strips during the last 5 minutes.

▶ When the flames in the barbecue have died and the coals are glowing, put the meat on the grill. Discard the marinade. Cook until the meat is done to your liking. Small skirt steaks will take about 10 to 15 minutes; flank steak will take longer.

▶ While the meat is cooking, warm the tortillas by wrapping them in a damp towel and putting them in a 350°F oven for about 10 minutes. Slice the beef thinly, then serve wrapped in tortillas with the sautéed onions and bell peppers and the salsa.

Chicken Enchiladas with Green Chile Sauce

Makes 6 servings

These enchiladas are not as spicy as the red ones because the Green Chile Sauce is mellowed by the addition of sour cream. Sliced fresh avocado makes a good garnish.

INGREDIENTS

¾ cup sour cream
3 cups Green Chile Sauce (page 32)
oil for frying
12 corn tortillas
2½ cups shredded cooked chicken
4 cups grated Jack cheese

METHOD

▶ Preheat the oven to 350°F. Have ready a large, shallow baking dish, such as a 13 x 9 x 2-inch cake pan. Stir the sour cream into the Green Chile Sauce, then pour into a wide, shallow dish.

▶ The process here is to fry the tortillas, dip them in the sauce, fill them with chicken and cheese, roll them, and place them in the baking dish. Set up the utensils and ingredients so you can do this like an assembly line.

▶ Pour oil into a skillet to a depth of ¼ to ½ inch. Heat until hot, but not smoking, then add the first tortilla. Fry the tortilla just long enough to heat and soften it, 2 to 3 seconds per side. Hold the tortilla just above the skillet for a few moments so excess oil can drain off. The heat under the skillet should be high enough to reheat the oil after each tortilla, but not so high that it overheats and smokes while you are assembling each enchilada.

▶ Working quickly, dip the tortilla in the sauce so both sides are immersed. It's okay if not very much adheres. Now remove the

tortilla and lay it flat. Spread 3 tbsp shredded chicken in a thin line up the center of the tortilla and sprinkle 2 to 3 tbsp grated cheese over it. If the tortilla does not have much green sauce on it, dab a little over the filling. Tightly roll the enchilada into a cylinder and put it, seam-side down, in the baking dish.

▶ Repeat the process until you have used up the tortillas and chicken, squeezing the enchiladas into a single layer in the baking dish, if possible.

▶ Spoon the remaining sauce over the enchiladas, then sprinkle over the remaining cheese. Bake, uncovered, for 15 minutes. Serve immediately.

Beef Enchiladas with Red Chile Sauce

Makes 6 servings

Enchiladas, one of Mexico's most popular dishes, are a combination of meat, cheese and sauce rolled up in a soft tortilla and baked. I like to use grilled meat – such as leftover Salsa-marinated Flank Steak (page 108) – because it gives them extra flavor, but any cooked and shredded beef will do. To counteract the heat of the Red Chile Sauce, serve sour cream on the side.

INGREDIENTS

2¹/₂ cups shredded cooked beef
²/₃ cup chopped green onions
3¹/₂ cups Red Chile Sauce (page 33)
4 cups grated Cheddar cheese
oil for frying
12 corn tortillas
sour cream

METHOD

▶ Preheat the oven to 350°F. Have ready a large, shallow baking dish, such as a 13 x 9 x 2-inch cake pan.

▶ Mix together the beef, green onions and 1 cup sauce. Pour the remaining sauce into a wide, shallow dish.

▶ The process here is to fry the tortillas, dip them in red sauce, fill them with the beef mixture and the cheese, roll them, and place them in the baking dish. Set up the utensils and ingredients so you can do this like an assembly line.

▶ Pour oil into a skillet to a depth of ¹/₄ to ¹/₂ inch. Heat until hot, but not smoking, then add the first tortilla. Fry the tortilla just long enough to heat and soften it, 2 to 3 seconds per side. Hold the tortilla just above the skillet for a few moments so excess oil can drain off. The heat under the skillet should be high enough to reheat the oil after each tortilla, but not so high that it overheats and smokes while you are assembling each enchilada.

▶ Working quickly, dip the tortilla in the sauce so both sides are immersed. Remove the tortilla and let excess sauce drip back into the dish. Lay the tortilla flat. Spread 3 tbsp of the beef mixture in a thin line up the center of the tortilla, then sprinkle 2 to 3 tbsp grated cheese over the beef. Tightly roll the enchilada into a cylinder and put it, seam-side down, in the baking dish.

▶ Repeat the process with the remaining tortillas and beef, squeezing the enchiladas into a single layer in the baking dish, if possible.

▶ Spoon the remaining sauce over the enchiladas, then sprinkle the remaining cheese over. Bake, uncovered, for 15 minutes. Serve immediately, with sour cream.

100

Tostadas

Each of these recipes make one tostada

Tostadas began life simply, as crisp, flat tortillas topped with beans, perhaps some meat, shredded lettuce or cabbage, a wedge of tomato, and sometimes cheese and a slice of avocado. Salsa was served on the side. In many restaurants, tostadas have evolved into enormous salads, served in huge bowls of deep-fried flour tortillas. Besides the traditional fillings, they are often made with more exotic ingredients.

At home, tostadas can be a way of using leftovers for a one-person dinner, or they can be the centerpiece of a casual dinner party. The method is the same.

Special equipment is needed to make flour tortillas into bowls, so it is best to keep it simple and stick to corn tortillas that are fried until crisp and laid flat on the plate. If you don't want to parcel out tortillas one by one as they come from the skillet, they can be kept in a warm oven for a short time, but really can't be prepared more than 10 or 15 minutes before eating.

INGREDIENTS FOR THE BASE

tortillas
vegetable oil

METHOD

▶ To fry tortillas, heat ¼ inch of oil in a skillet. Add a tortilla and cook until crisp, about 1 minute. Drain.

▶ The choice of tostada toppings is unlimited, but here are three combinations to start with. Use your imagination and your own taste to come up with others.

▶ Layer the ingredients on the fried tortilla in the order listed.

INGREDIENTS FOR THE TOPPINGS

TRADITIONAL

¼ cup Chorizo-Bean Dip (page 53) or refried beans
⅓ cup shredded cooked beef or chicken
¾ cup chopped lettuce
⅓ cup grated Cheddar cheese
tomato and avocado wedges
2 to 3 tbsp Salsa Cruda (pages 18–19)

MODERN

1 cup torn lettuce
½ to ⅔ cup Grilled Chicken (page 110) or Salsa-marinated Flank Steak (page 109), cubed
½ cup chunks of Jack cheese
6 black olives
tomato wedges
2 to 3 tbsp Avocado Salsa (page 22)

EXOTIC

⅔ cup Mango Salsa (page 46) or Nectarine Salsa (page 45)
6 Grilled Shrimp (page 119)

▶ Cut large shrimp into bite-sized pieces. Mix with the salsa, then mound onto the tortillas.

Black Bean Chiles Rellenos

Makes 6 first-course servings or
3 main-course servings

Chiles rellenos means stuffed chiles, and in this recipe they are stuffed with spicy black beans and cheese. The rellenos are dipped in beaten egg, then quickly fried – a messy procedure, but worth it. The chiles can be stuffed in advance, then fried at the last minute. Use Anaheims for a mild dish, poblanos for spicier fare, and serve salsa or Red or Green Chile Sauce (pages 32–3) on the side.

INGREDIENTS

6 large Anaheim or poblano chiles
6 thick slices Jack cheese, about 1 x 4 inches
about 1¼ cups Chorizo-Bean Dip (page 53)
about ⅔ cup cornmeal for dredging
3 eggs, separated

2 tbsp flour
¼ tsp salt
vegetable oil for frying

METHOD

▶ Broil or grill the whole chiles until skin is blistered and partly blackened. Place the chiles in a plastic bag for 10 minutes so their steam can loosen the skins. Remove the skins. Cut a slit along the length of each chile, and carefully remove the seeds.

▶ Put a slice of cheese in each chile, then lightly stuff with the bean filling. Dredge the stuffed chile in cornmeal.

▶ In a medium bowl, beat the egg whites until soft peaks form. In a small bowl, beat the egg yolks with the flour and salt. Fold the yolks into the whites.

▶ Pour oil into a large skillet to a depth of ½ inch and heat. Dip each chile into the egg mixture, and use a small rubber spatula to be sure it is thoroughly coated. (*Note:* The fried egg coating will seal the relleno.) Put the relleno in the hot oil and fry until golden, about 1 minute a side. You should fry only 2 rellenos at a time, 3 if you have a very large skillet. Do not crowd them.

▶ Drain briefly and serve immediately.

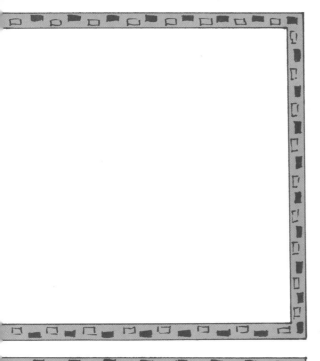

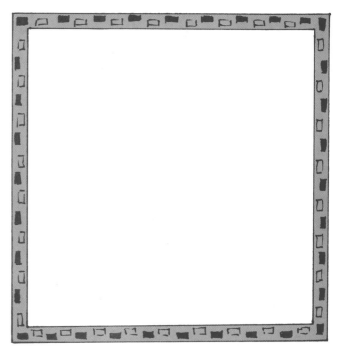

meat dishes

Salsa Chicken

Jerk Chicken

Machaca

Salsa-marinated Flank Steak

Grilled Chicken

Roast Pork with Chorizo-Rice Stuffing

Chimichurri

Hamburgers

Lamb with Black Bean Salsa

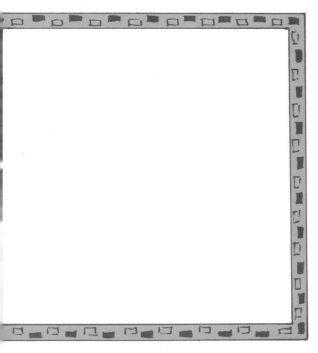

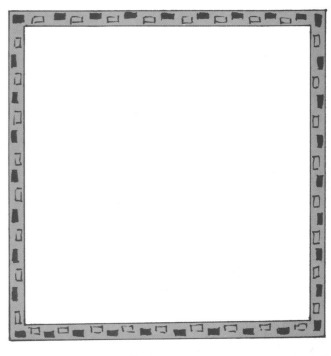

Salsa Chicken

Makes 4 servings

Although this recipe calls for boneless chicken breasts, you can use other parts if you adjust the cooking time. You can reduce the cooking time by cutting the chicken into strips or chunks.

INGREDIENTS

¼ cup flour
1 tsp ground cumin
1 tsp paprika
½ tsp salt
¼ tsp pepper
4 boneless chicken breast halves
1 to 2 tbsp vegetable oil
1 cup tomato-based salsa
about ½ cup chicken broth (optional)

METHOD

▶ Mix the flour with the cumin, paprika, salt and pepper. Sprinkle it over the chicken breasts and turn the chicken so all sides are coated with the mixture. Heat the oil in a large skillet. Add the chicken pieces and brown them on both sides, then stir in the salsa. If the salsa is very thick, add the chicken stock. Simmer the chicken until cooked through, 20 to 30 minutes, occasionally spooning the salsa over the top. Serve over rice or noodles.

Jerk Chicken

Makes 6 servings

Jerk chicken is a Jamaican dish that features the hottest chiles available – the Caribbean Scotch bonnet or its cousin from the Yucatan, the habanero. The chicken is marinated in a paste made of Fiery Habanero Salsa, mustard and herbs, then grilled slowly over indirect heat. The result is very spicy, but if you want truly incendiary chicken, as some jerk chicken is, add another habanero chile to the paste. In order to cook the chicken long and slow, bone-in pieces such as breasts or thighs are recommended. However, other parts or boneless breasts can also be used if they are carefully watched during cooking. Serve with a fruit salsa, Avocado Salsa (page 22), or a black bean salsa.

INGREDIENTS

½ cup Fiery Habanero Salsa (page 38)
2 tbsp prepared yellow mustard
1 tbsp dried rosemary or 2 tbsp fresh
1 tbsp dried basil or 3 tbsp fresh
1 tbsp dried thyme or 3 tbsp fresh
2 tbsp fresh lime or orange juice
3 cloves garlic
1 tsp allspice
1 tsp salt
½ tsp pepper
6 chicken breasts or 8 to 10 chicken thighs

METHOD

► Process all the ingredients except the chicken in a blender or food processor until you have a thick paste. Smear the paste all over the chicken (don't use your bare fingers!), including under the skin if you leave the skin on. Refrigerate for at least 2 hours and up to 12 hours.

► Ignite the coals in a barbecue kettle. When the flames have died and the coals are glowing, put the chicken on the greased grill as far from the coals as possible. Cover and let cook. Check the coals every 15 minutes or so, and add new coals if necessary. Turn the chicken once or twice, until the meat is cooked through and the juices run clear when it is pierced with a skewer. This could take as little as 20 minutes for wings or boneless breasts if the fire is hot, or an hour or more for large, bone-in pieces and a cooler fire.

107

Machaca

Makes 6 to 8 servings

Machaca is a shredded dried beef dish from northern Mexico. Traditional recipes call for the beef to be air-dried for several days before it is cooked and shredded, but in this recipe, it is simply simmered long and slow, then shredded and baked. Most of the work can be done a day in advance. Serve Machaca with warm flour tortillas and Black Bean-Corn Salsa (page 36) or any salsa of your choice. Leftovers are marvelous in Quesadillas (page 96) or scrambled eggs.

Ingredients

3-pound beef roast (chuck, brisket or other cut)
1 tbsp ground cumin
2 tsp dried oregano
1 tsp salt
1 tsp pepper
1 to 2 tbsp vegetable oil
1 onion, peeled and cut into wedges
2 to 3 cups Salsa Cruda (pages 18–19) or Chipotle Salsa (page 34)
2 eggs, lightly beaten with a fork

Method

▶ Trim any excess fat from the beef. Mix together the cumin, oregano, salt and pepper, and rub this mixture over the surface of the roast. Let sit for 30 minutes to allow the flavors to develop.

▶ Heat the oil in a deep skillet or Dutch oven. Add the meat and brown it on all sides. Add the onion and water to a depth of 1 inch. Bring the water to a boil, then cover the pan and reduce the heat to a simmer. Or you can transfer the pot to the oven and cook at 350°F. Allow the meat to cook until it is tender and falling from the bone, about 2½ hours. Check occasionally during cooking and add more water if needed.

▶ When the meat is done, cut it into several large pieces and let it cool slightly. When it is cool enough to handle, use 2 forks to pull the meat apart into shreds. It is easier to shred the meat while it is still very warm.

▶ Spread the shredded meat on a large baking sheet and bake in a preheated 350°F oven, 12 to 15 minutes, turning once or twice, until it is dry. The meat may be prepared in advance to this point, then refrigerated until just before serving time.

▶ Put the meat in a large skillet with the salsa and cook over medium heat. Let it simmer for about 10 minutes so that any excess moisture in the salsa evaporates. Add the beaten eggs and cook, stirring well, so there are strands of egg mixed through the meat. Serve immediately with warm flour tortillas and salsa.

Salsa-marinated Flank Steak

Makes 4 to 6 servings

A salsa marinade adds flavor to flank steak, or any other thick cut of beef that you like to barbecue. Grill the beef, then slice it thinly. Serve with salad, warm tortillas, and a choice of salsas – perhaps Avocado Salsa (page 22) and Grilled Salsa (page 26).

INGREDIENTS

1/3 cup cooked or puréed tomato-based salsa, such as Basic Cooked Salsa (page 32) or Grilled Salsa (page 26)
1/3 cup dry red wine
1/3 cup vegetable oil
3 cloves garlic, minced
2 pounds flank steak or other cut of beef

METHOD

▶ Combine all the ingredients except the beef and mix well. Put the beef in a sturdy plastic food-storage bag. Add the marinade to the bag and make sure the beef is fully coated. Tie the end of the bag, then refrigerate for at least 4 hours and up to 24 hours, turning occasionally.

▶ About 90 minutes before you want to eat, start a fire in the barbecue kettle. When the flames have died and the coals are glowing, remove the meat from the bag and place it on an oiled grill directly over the coals. Grilling over the coals will char the outside of the steak while the inside cooks slowly. However,

if drips cause too many flare-ups, you may wish to move the meat off to the side and cover the kettle.

▶ Cooking time will depend on the thickness of the meat, the distance above the coals, and the heat of the coals. For meat that is 1½ inches thick, cook for at least 7 minutes a side, then check whether it is done. It may take as long as 15 minutes a side.

▶ When the meat is done, remove it from the grill and let it sit for 10 to 20 minutes for ease of carving. Cutting against the grain, slice the meat thinly and serve.

109

Grilled Chicken

Makes 4 servings

In this recipe, chicken breasts are marinated in a simple, spicy, citrus marinade, then grilled over hot coals. It is a dish that tastes excellent hot or cold. It's also delicious cut into chunks and served on a green salad, topped with salsa – Avocado Salsa (page 22) and Nectarine Salsa (page 45) are particularly good.

INGREDIENTS

½ cup olive oil
2 tbsp fresh lime juice
3 tbsp fresh orange juice
2 cloves garlic, minced
1 tbsp chopped fresh cilantro
¼ tsp hot pepper sauce
4 boneless chicken breast halves, with or
    without skin
1 tsp freshly ground black pepper
½ to 1 cup salsa of your choice

110

METHOD

▶ Make a marinade by mixing together all the ingredients except the chicken, the salsa and the black pepper. Put the chicken in a plastic or glass bowl and pour the marinade over it. Turn the chicken breasts so they are thoroughly coated, then let marinate, refrigerated, for at least 6 hours or overnight. Turn the chicken 2 or 3 times while it is marinating. Just before grilling, sprinkle with the black pepper.

▶ About an hour before serving time, start the fire in the barbecue. When the flames have died, and the coals are glowing and covered with white ash (about 40 minutes), put the chicken breasts on the greased grill over the coals. Grill, turning once, until the chicken is cooked through, about 12 minutes, depending on the thickness of the meat and the distance from the coals. Serve with salsa on top or on the side.

New Mexico chiles in their red and green stages.

Roast Pork with Chorizo-Rice Stuffing

Makes 6 servings

Pork loin is stuffed with a spicy chorizo-rice stuffing, then slathered with salsa and roasted. Use any vegetable salsa of your choice. Fiery Habanero Salsa (page 38) infuses the meat with the heat of the chiles, while milder salsas let the other flavors show through. Roast Jalapeño Salsa (page 16) is a good, though messy choice. Chunkier salsas, such as Salsa Cruda III (page 19), have a tendency to fall off.

INGREDIENTS

¹/₄ tsp salt
2 tsp olive oil or butter
1 cup white rice
6 to 8 ounces chorizo sausage
¹/₂ cup chopped onion
2 cloves garlic, minced
¹/₄ cup toasted pine nuts (see below)
2 to 2¹/₂-pound pork loin
1¹/₂ to 2 cups salsa

METHOD

▶ Preheat the oven to 350°F. Put 2 cups water in a small saucepan, add the salt and olive oil or butter and bring to a boil. Stir in the rice, cover and reduce the heat. Cook until the water has been absorbed and the rice is tender, 15 to 20 minutes.

▶ Meanwhile, crumble the chorizo into a small skillet. Cook over medium heat until the sausage is browned, 7 to 10 minutes, then remove with a slotted spoon and set aside. Discard all but 1 tbsp of fat. Reheat the fat and add the onion. Sauté for 5 minutes, then add the garlic and pine nuts, and cook for 1 minute longer. Remove from the heat. Mix the chorizo and the onion mixture into the cooked rice.

▶ Unroll the pork loin, or make several lengthwise cuts so that it opens as much as possible into a thick, flat piece. Spoon some rice mixture into the center of the loin, then reroll the meat and tie with string. You will have some rice left over. Put it in a lightly greased baking dish, cover and set aside.

▶ Put the pork, cut side up, on a rack in a small roasting pan. Spread some of the salsa over the pork, coating it as much as possible, but make sure you have some salsa left over for basting. Put the roast in the oven and cook for approximately 1 hour, until the internal temperature measured with a meat thermometer reaches 160°F (although the meat is safe at 140°). Baste the meat at least once with the additional salsa. During the last 5 minutes of cooking, put the leftover rice stuffing in the oven.

▶ When the pork is done, remove it from the oven and let sit for 15 minutes before carving it into slices. Let the stuffing continue to cook while the pork rests.

To toast pine nuts: Spread them in a single layer on a baking sheet. Bake at 350°F for 5 to 10 minutes until they are golden brown. Watch pine nuts carefully as they burn very quickly.

112

Chimichurri

Makes 6 servings

Chimichurri is Argentinian barbecued beef served with a parsley-vinegar salsa. Beefsteaks (usually fillet, rib steaks or strip steaks) are marinated in a simple mixture, such as a saltwater brine, salt and lemon juice, or just salt and pepper. Sometimes they are marinated in Chimichurri Salsa. This salsa varies widely. Typically it is thinner than most salsas, and includes vinegar, olive oil, garlic, onion and parsley. However, lime juice or orange juice – especially sour orange – is frequently substituted for all or part of the vinegar. A small amount of oregano may take the place of parsley, and fresh or ground dried chiles are optional.

If you wish to marinate the beef in Chimichurri Salsa before cooking, make a double portion of salsa. Discard any excess marinade and serve the cooked beef with fresh Chimichurri Salsa. Marinade that has been in contact with raw beef should not be eaten unless it is boiled first.

INGREDIENTS

6 beefsteaks
salt and pepper
3 cloves garlic, minced
Chimichurri Salsa (recipe follows)

METHOD

▶ Sprinkle the beef with salt and pepper, then rub with the minced garlic. Allow to sit for an hour or longer in the refrigerator. Meanwhile, prepare the barbecue. When the barbecue coals are glowing and the flames have barely died, grill the meat until it is done to your liking. Serve with Chimichurri Salsa.

INGREDIENTS FOR CHIMICHURRI SALSA

³/₄ cup good-quality olive oil
¹/₄ cup red wine vinegar
³/₄ cup chopped fresh parsley
1 tsp dried oregano
1 jalapeño chile, chopped
5 cloves garlic, minced
2 tbsp minced onion
¹/₂ tsp salt
¹/₄ tsp pepper

METHOD

▶ Combine all the ingredients. You may chop them briefly in a food processor, if desired. Let sit for at least 30 minutes before serving.

Hamburgers

Makes 1 serving

Is there an ingredient that hasn't been tried on hamburgers? Salsa is a popular addition, either as a condiment or mixed in with the meat. Here are some ideas for combining salsa and hamburgers.

METHOD

▶ Mix 1 to 2 tbsp salsa with ⅓ pound ground beef before making into patties. Any tomato-based or tomatillo salsa is good, but Tomato-Mint Salsa (page 24) adds an unexpected twist. Roast Jalapeño Salsa (page 16) is also a good addition.

▶ Spoon salsa over the cooked meat or spread it on the bun. In addition to the above salsas, Sweet Red Pepper (page 20) and Olive Salsa (page 22) go well with hamburgers.

▶ Make an avocado burger by topping the cooked meat with Guacamole (page 17) or Avocado Salsa (page 22).

▶ For an unusual sandwich, serve the burger open-faced with Black Bean Salsa (page 26). Or for a tropical touch, try Pineapple-Ginger Salsa (page 42).

Lamb with Black Bean Salsa

Makes 6 servings

In this Brazilian-inspired dish, a leg of lamb is marinated, then roasted or grilled, and served with salsa. It is a relatively simple dish that requires a minimum of last-minute work.

INGREDIENTS

leg of lamb, about 5 pounds (see Note below)
⅓ cup olive oil
¼ cup red wine vinegar
2 tbsp fresh orange juice
4 cloves garlic, minced
1 tsp dried oregano
½ tsp dried rosemary
⅓ cup finely chopped onion
1½ cups Black Bean Salsa (page 26) or Black Bean-Papaya Salsa (page 46)

METHOD

▶ Put the lamb in a non-metallic dish. To make a marinade, combine all the remaining ingredients except the salsa. Pour the marinade over the lamb, making sure that the entire surface is coated. Marinate the lamb in the refrigerator for at least 2 hours and up to 24 hours, turning it occasionally and spooning marinade over it.

▶ Roast the lamb in a 350°F oven or over a grill. Lamb is cooked rare when it reaches an internal temperature of 140°F (test with a meat thermometer) – about 20 minutes per pound in the oven, considerably less time on a grill. Lamb is traditionally served rare or medium rare (about 150°F). It is easier to carve if it is allowed to rest for about 20 minutes after it comes out of the oven. Serve with the salsa.

Note: Weight is for bone-in meat. If you plan to grill the lamb, ask the butcher to remove the bone and butterfly the meat so it lies relatively flat.

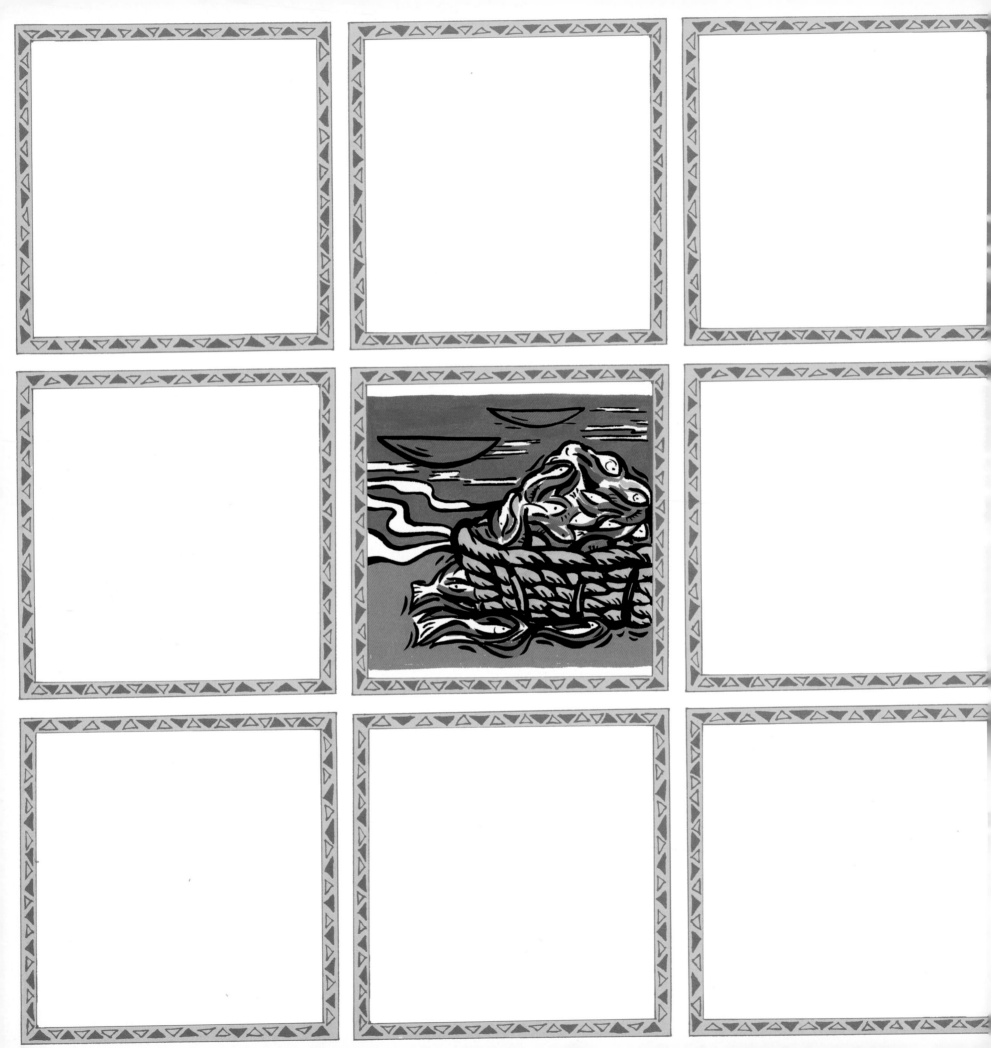

seafood dishes

Ceviche
Grilled Shrimp
Red Snapper Veracruz
Grilled Clams
Shrimp in Chipotle Salsa
Grilled Salmon
Shrimp-stuffed Green Peppers

Ceviche

Makes 2 to 3 servings

In this specialty dish from Central and South America, raw fish or shellfish is marinated in spices and lemon or lime juice until the citrus "cooks" the seafood. This version uses a habanero chile for extra heat. (If you can't find a habanero, substitute 2 serrano chiles.) Ceviche can be served like shrimp cocktail, or spooned over lettuce for a salad. Be sure to use extremely fresh, high-quality seafood.

INGREDIENTS

½ pound white fish fillets, shrimp or scallops, or a combination
¾ cup fresh lime juice
1 cup Salsa Cruda III (page 19)
½ sweet red pepper, cut into strips
1 habanero chile, cut crosswise into thin rings
1 tbsp white vinegar
2 tbsp olive oil

METHOD

▶ Clean the seafood as needed; peel and devein shrimp, if using. Cut into bite-sized pieces. If you are using large shrimp, cut them into 2 or 3 pieces so the lime juice can penetrate evenly. Mix the remaining ingredients in a non-metallic bowl, then stir in the seafood pieces so all are evenly coated. Refrigerate for at least 6 hours, until the seafood turns opaque, as if cooked.

Grilled Shrimp

Makes 4 main-course servings or
6 first-course servings

Marinated and grilled shrimp served with salsa make a delicious appetizer or light main course. For variety, serve them with Grilled Clams (page 120) and two or three salsas. Try any traditional tomato-based salsa, one of the corn salsas, or Nectarine Salsa (page 45).

INGREDIENTS

1 pound medium to large shrimp, shelled
    and deveined
1/2 cup olive oil
3 cloves garlic, minced
3 tbsp fresh lime juice
2 tbsp chopped fresh basil or 2 tsp dried
1 tsp red pepper flakes

METHOD

► Place the shrimp in a glass or plastic bowl. Mix together all the remaining ingredients. Pour this marinade over the shrimp and stir, making sure that all the shrimp are thoroughly coated. Marinate, refrigerated, for 2 to 4 hours, stirring 2 or 3 times.

► About 45 minutes before you want to eat, start the barbecue fire. If you plan to use wooden skewers, soak them in water for at least 30 minutes so they don't burn easily. A few minutes before the coals are ready, thread the shrimp loosely on the skewers. If they are crammed together, they will not cook evenly.

► When the flames have died down and the coals are glowing and covered with white ash, place the shrimp on the greased grill. They will cook quickly, especially if dripping marinade causes flare-ups, so they need to be closely watched. Grill, turning once, until cooked through, about 2 to 4 minutes a side, depending on the size of the shrimp and the distance from the coals. The shrimp will lose their translucency and turn an opaque white-pink. Do not overcook them, or they will get tough. Serve with salsas of your choice.

Red Snapper Veracruz

Makes 4 servings

In this version of a traditional Mexican recipe the fish is fried briefly, then simmered in a tomato salsa. It is good served over plain rice or on its own.

INGREDIENTS

4 fillets of red snapper, about 6 ounces each
salt and pepper
4 tbsp flour
2 tbsp vegetable oil
2 cups Salsa Cruda I (page 18) or Salsa
*   Cruda III (page 19)*

½ sweet red pepper, cut into strips
1 or 2 jalapeño chiles, seeded and cut
*   into rings*
¼ cup chopped green onions
1 tbsp chopped fresh cilantro

METHOD

▶ Season the fish fillets with salt and pepper, then dust with the flour. Heat the oil in a skillet, add the fillets and cook them quickly, so that each side is lightly browned.

▶ Add the salsa, red pepper and jalapeños to the pan. Simmer over low heat, spooning the salsa over the fish. Cook until the fish flakes easily, about 10 minutes per inch of thickness.

▶ Put the fish onto serving plates, spooning salsa, red pepper strips and jalapeño rings over each piece. Garnish with the green onions and cilantro.

Grilled Clams

Few dishes beat Grilled Clams for simplicity. Serve them as an appetizer, cooking them on the grill before the main course goes on the fire, or as a main course by themselves or with Grilled Shrimp (page 119). They are good with Salsa Cruda I (page 18), Nectarine Salsa (page 45), or Corn Salsa (page 21) on the side.

INGREDIENTS

4 to 6 clams per person for an appetizer;
*   12 per person for a main course*
salsa of your choice
melted butter and garlic (optional)

METHOD

▶ Scrub the clam shells clean under cool running water. Discard any clams that are not tightly closed or don't close tightly under the running water. When the barbecue coals are glowing and the flames have died, place the clams on the grill over the coals. A screen for cooking small items is handy, to be sure the clams don't slip through the grill. Cook until the clam shells pop open, 5 to 10 minutes.

▶ In addition to salsa, serve a bowl of butter melted with a little garlic for dipping.

Shrimp in Chipotle Salsa

Makes 4 servings

Lime-marinated shrimp are sautéed, then cooked briefly in Chipotle Salsa, which imparts its hot, smoky flavor to the shrimp. Serve them on their own or over plain white rice. If you don't have time to make Chipotle Salsa, make Winter Salsa II (page 39), which uses canned chipotle chiles, while the shrimp are marinating.

INGREDIENTS

⅓ cup olive oil
⅓ cup fresh lime juice
3 cloves garlic, minced
1¼ pounds medium or large shrimp, peeled and deveined
1½ cups Chipotle Salsa (page 34)
½ tsp salt

METHOD

▶ Mix together 2 tbsp olive oil, the lime juice and garlic to make a marinade. Put the shrimp in a glass or other non-reactive bowl. Pour the marinade over the shrimp, and toss so that all the pieces are coated. Let marinate for 30 minutes.

▶ Heat the remaining oil in a large skillet. Remove the shrimp from the bowl, reserving the marinade. Add the shrimp to the oil and sauté quickly over medium heat for about 1½ minutes. Remove the shrimp and set aside. Add the Chipotle Salsa to the remaining oil and fry it, stirring almost constantly, for 5 minutes. Add the marinade and salt, and cook for another 2 minutes. Return the shrimp to the skillet and cook for about 2 minutes longer, just long enough to cook through the shrimp and let them absorb some of the salsa flavors.

121

Grilled Salmon

Makes 4 servings

Salmon is marinated in a chile vinaigrette, then broiled or grilled. It is delicious served with Black Bean-Corn Salsa (page 36), or with a fruit salsa. This recipe also works well with the more substantial white fish like halibut and swordfish.

Ingredients

1 poblano chile
½ cup olive oil
2 tbsp red wine vinegar
2 cloves garlic, peeled
1 tbsp chopped fresh cilantro
1½ pounds salmon fillet
salsa of your choice

Method

▶ Cut the poblano chile in quarters lengthwise, remove the stem, seeds and veins. Broil chile, skin side up, until skin is blackened. Put the chile in a small plastic bag or pouch of aluminum foil for 10 minutes, then peel off the skin. It's okay if a few bits of blackened skin remain. Put the chile in a blender or food processor with all the remaining ingredients except the salmon and salsa. Purée.

▶ Put the salmon in a shallow glass or other non-reactive dish and pour the purée over it. Turn the salmon to make sure it is completely coated, then marinate in the refrigerator for 1 to 4 hours.

▶ Preheat the broiler, or start a fire in the barbecue and wait until the flames have died and the coals are glowing. Place the salmon on a lightly oiled broiler pan and put under the broiler, or place on an oiled grill over the coals. Cook, turning once, until barely cooked through, about 8 minutes total, depending on the thickness of the fish. Serve with salsa on top or on the side.

122

Shrimp-stuffed Green Peppers

Makes 4 servings

These bell peppers are stuffed with a tasty mixture of rice, shrimp, salsa and sour cream, then baked. They make an excellent lunch or light supper dish. For extra flavor, cook the shrimp in Chipotle Salsa (page 34).

INGREDIENTS

4 green bell peppers
2 cups cooked white rice
8 ounces cooked shrimp, cleaned and cut into bite-sized pieces
1 cup Salsa Cruda (see pages 18–19)
1 cup sour cream
¼ cup chopped green onion
½ tsp ground cumin
1 tsp salt (optional)

METHOD

▶ Preheat the oven to 350°F. Lightly oil a shallow baking dish, about 9 x 9 inches.

▶ Cut the tops off the bell peppers and reserve. Wash the peppers and clean out the seeds and membranes. Bring a large saucepan of water to a boil, and add the bell peppers. Boil for 2 minutes, then remove and drain.

▶ Make the stuffing by combining all the remaining ingredients, adding the salt, if the rice was cooked without salt. Gently stuff this mixture into the peppers, then stand them in the baking dish. Put the tops back on the peppers and bake for about 40 minutes, until they are tender but not collapsing.

vegetarian dishes

Polenta with Black Bean Salsa
Huevos Rancheros
Deluxe Huevos Rancheros
Cheese Salsa Omelet
Southwestern Frittata
Cornmeal Pancakes
with Black Beans
Double-Salsa with Black-eyed Peas

Polenta with Black Bean Salsa

Makes about 6 servings

This is a hybrid dish, combining Italian polenta with Southwestern Black Bean Salsa. Serve it for lunch or a light dinner. The polenta must be prepared in advance. Traditional polenta – a coarse grind of cornmeal similar to grits – needs cooking for at least 30 minutes, but now quick-cooking polentas are available; however, they taste better if you cook them for 10 minutes longer than recommended on the package.

INGREDIENTS

Polenta (recipe follows)
olive oil for frying or grilling
12 ounces Cheddar cheese, thinly sliced
1 1/2 cups Black Bean Salsa (page 26)

METHOD

► Cut the polenta into slices about 1 1/2 inches thick. If you are going to grill it, lightly brush the cut edges with olive oil. If you are going to fry it, heat 1 tbsp olive oil in a skillet.

► When the oil is hot, or when the barbecue coals are glowing and the flames have died, put the polenta slices on the heat. Cook until the bottom is golden (if frying) or charred with grill marks, about 3 minutes. Turn the polenta and put the sliced cheese on top. Cook until the underneath is golden or charred. (*Note:* If you are frying the polenta, the cheese will melt more readily if you use a lid on the skillet. Add more oil if necessary before frying next batch of polenta.)

► Remove the polenta from the heat. Spoon the Black Bean Salsa over the top, and serve.

INGREDIENTS FOR POLENTA

2 tsp salt
2 cups polenta

METHOD

► Lightly oil a loaf pan, about 9 x 5 inches. Bring 6 cups water and the salt to a boil in a large saucepan. Slowly add the polenta, stirring constantly and watching for lumps. Cook over low heat, stirring almost constantly, 30 minutes or so, until the polenta forms a thick mass that pulls cleanly away from the sides of pan. Pour the polenta into the loaf pan and smooth the top. Let it cool for at least 30 minutes before turning out.

Huevos Rancheros

Makes 4 servings

Huevos Rancheros is a traditional Mexican breakfast dish, with as many variations as there are families. This is a simple version made with tortillas, fried eggs, cheese and salsa. Any tomato or tomatillo salsa is suitable, or try a black bean salsa for a change. For a heartier breakfast, fry 2 eggs per serving. Since this dish is made in steps, use heatproof plates, and keep them warm in the oven between steps.

INGREDIENTS

1 to 1¹/₂ cups salsa of your choice
oil for frying

4 corn tortillas
4 eggs
1 cup grated Cheddar cheese
chopped green onions and cilantro for
  garnish

METHOD

▶ Heat the oven to 150°F and put the plates in to warm. Warm the salsa in a small saucepan over low heat.

▶ Heat a little oil in a skillet. Fry the tortillas, one at a time, for a few seconds per side, just enough to soften. Drain each tortilla and put on a plate in the oven.

▶ Discard all but 1 tbsp oil. Keep the heat at medium. Break the eggs onto saucers, and slide them into the hot oil. Cook for 2 or 3 minutes until the yolks are set, spooning hot oil over the top of the eggs or covering the pan to keep the heat in. If desired, turn the eggs and cook for about 30 seconds longer.

▶ Put 1 egg on each tortilla. Top with salsa and sprinkle the cheese over the top. Garnish with green onions and cilantro.

Deluxe Huevos Rancheros

Makes 4 servings

This is a heartier version than the previous one, beginning with a simple quesadilla that is topped with beans. The eggs are poached in salsa. This version needs a fairly liquid tomato salsa, such as any Salsa Cruda (pages 18–19), or Basic Cooked Salsa (page 32). For extra flavor, try Chipotle Salsa (page 34) or Winter Salsa II (page 39), which is made with chipotle chiles.

INGREDIENTS

8 flour tortillas
2 cups grated Jack cheese
vegetable oil or melted butter
1 cup refried beans
2 to 3 cups salsa of your choice
8 eggs
chopped tomatoes and black olives for
*   garnish*

128

METHOD

► Preheat the oven to 350°F. Lightly oil 2 baking sheets.

► Place 4 tortillas on the baking sheets and sprinkle each one with ⅓ cup cheese, evenly spread over the entire tortilla. Place a second tortilla on top of the cheese and press down. Lightly brush the top of the second tortilla with oil or melted butter. Bake for 5 to 8 minutes until the cheese is barely melted. Reduce the oven heat to warm.

► Fry the beans in a scant amount of oil, just to heat through. Spread ¼ cup of beans on top of each quesadilla. Return the quesadillas to the oven to keep warm.

► Put half the salsa in a medium skillet and heat for 2 to 3 minutes. Break 4 eggs onto saucers and slide them into the salsa. Cover and poach for about 3 minutes. Put 2 eggs each on 2 quesadillas and divide the sauce between them. Repeat with the remaining 4 eggs and salsa. Or you may poach all the eggs at the same time in 2 skillets.

► Sprinkle the remaining cheese over the eggs. Garnish with some chopped tomatoes and olives.

Mexican children enjoying tortillas.

Cheese Salsa Omelet

Makes 1 serving

Eggs and salsa are a great combination, and here are two omelets that incorporate the salsa right into the cooking. Use your imagination to create other variations.

INGREDIENTS

2 or 3 eggs
pinch of salt
few drops of hot pepper sauce
butter or oil for frying
¼ cup grated Cheddar cheese
2 tbsp tomato-based salsa, plus extra to serve
2 slices of avocado

METHOD

▶ Beat the eggs, salt and hot pepper sauce together with a fork just until blended. Heat about 1 to 2 teaspoons butter or oil in a 7- or 8-inch skillet, pour in the eggs and shake the pan a little so they spread evenly across the bottom. As the egg cooks and curls around the edges, lift the edge slightly with a fork or knife and tilt the pan so that the uncooked egg runs from the center of the omelet and under the cooked egg. Continue lifting and tilting until all the liquid egg has run over the edges and set, but the center is still soft. Sprinkle the cheese in a 2-inch wide band up the center,

then spoon the salsa over the cheese. Use a spatula to fold one-third of the omelet over the cheese. Now, as you ease the omelet out of the pan and onto a serving plate, fold the other third over the center. Garnish with the avocado and serve with extra salsa on the side.

Variation: Instead of salsa, spread 3 tbsp warmed Hot Bean Dip (page 52) up the center of the omelet. Sprinkle cheese over the beans, then top with 2 tbsp sour cream.

Southwestern Frittata

Makes 4 to 6 servings

A frittata is a one-dish meal of eggs, cheese, and fried potatoes, seasoned with salsa. It is similar to an omelet, but is baked in the oven and is large enough to serve several people. This recipe is particularly good with any of the salsas in which grilled or roast chiles or bell peppers are the primary ingredient, such as Roast Jalapeño Salsa (page 16) or Sweet Red Pepper Salsa (page 20). For this dish, you will need an ovenproof skillet with a 6- to 8-cup capacity. If you don't have such a skillet, fry the potatoes, onions and salsa, then transfer them to a casserole dish and add the remaining ingredients.

INGREDIENTS

vegetable oil for frying
2 cups peeled and diced potato
1 cup chopped onion
1 cup salsa of your choice, plus extra for
* serving*
1 cup grated Jack or Cheddar cheese
6 eggs
2 tbsp milk
1 tsp salt
¼ tsp pepper

METHOD

▶ Heat the oil in a skillet. Add the potato and onion and fry until golden, about 15 minutes. (Or you can boil the potatoes until they are barely tender, then dice and fry.) Add the salsa. If you are using a tomato-based salsa, let it simmer for 5 minutes or so to cook off any excess liquid. Remove from the heat. Preheat the oven to 400°F.

▶ Sprinkle the grated cheese over the potatoes and onions. Break the eggs into a bowl, add the milk, salt and pepper and beat lightly. Pour this mixture over the potatoes. Bake the frittata in the skillet until the eggs have puffed up, the center is set and the edges are golden, about 15 minutes. Cut into wedges and serve with additional salsa on the side.

Cornmeal Pancakes with Black Beans

Makes 15 to 18 4-inch pancakes, or 6 to 8 servings

This savory dish, excellent for brunch, features thin, crisp-edged cornmeal pancakes topped with spicy black beans, salsa and sour cream. The beans, salsa and pancake batter can be made the night before.

INGREDIENTS

Cornmeal Pancakes (recipe follows)
2 to 2¹/₂ cups Hot Bean Dip (made with vegetarian refried beans)
1 cup Salsa Cruda of choice (pages 18–19)
1¹/₂ cups sour cream

METHOD

▶ Make the pancakes as directed below. Heat the bean dip. When the pancakes are cooked, spoon some bean dip on each, add a little salsa, and top with a dollop of sour cream.

INGREDIENTS FOR CORNMEAL PANCAKES

¹/₂ cup flour
³/₄ cup cornmeal
1 tsp baking powder
1 tsp baking soda
1 tsp salt
1¹/₂ cups buttermilk
3 tbsp melted butter
2 eggs, lightly beaten with fork
oil for frying

METHOD

▶ Combine the dry ingredients in a medium bowl. Mix together the buttermilk, melted butter and eggs, then stir into the dry ingredients. Mix by hand until the ingredients are combined but the batter is still slightly lumpy.

▶ Heat a scant amount of oil in a skillet, barely enough to coat the pan lightly. Spoon in small amounts of batter, tilting the skillet so the batter spreads out to make thin pancakes. Cook over medium heat until the underside is golden brown, then turn and cook the other side. Don't crowd the pancakes. Use 2 skillets at once if you wish. Add oil as needed, but only in tiny amounts.

Double-Salsa with Black-eyed Peas

Makes 6 to 8 servings

This is a vegetarian version of Hopping John, the black-eyed pea and rice dish that Southerners eat for good luck on New Year's Day. Instead of simmering the peas with ham, mix the cooked peas with Chipotle Salsa, which gives them a hot, smoky flavor that substitutes well for meat. The rice and pea mixture is topped with a chunky raw salsa that adds color, a crunchy texture, and the flavor of tomatoes and onions.

Ingredients

2 cups dried black-eyed peas
1¹⁄₂ to 2 cups Chipotle Salsa (page 34)
1 to 2 tsp salt
¹⁄₂ tsp pepper
4 cups cooked white rice
about 2 cups Salsa Cruda III (page 19)
¹⁄₃ cup chopped green onions

Method

► Sort through the peas for pebbles or other debris, then put the peas in a large saucepan with 2 quarts water. Bring to a boil, cover and boil for 2 minutes, then turn off the heat and let the peas sit for an hour.

► Drain and rinse the peas. Rinse the saucepan, then put the peas back in the pan and add enough water to cover them by 3 inches. Bring to a boil, then cook over low heat until most of the water has evaporated and the peas are tender. Add the Chipotle Salsa, salt, and pepper during the last few minutes of cooking.

► Put the rice in bowls and spoon the peas over the rice. Stir the green onions into the Salsa Cruda, then top the beans with this mixture.

133

desserts

Honey-Ginger Peach Salsa
Tropical Dessert Salsa
Fruit Salsa Romanoff
Banana Salsa
Salsa Ice Cream
Sopapillas
Cookie Cups with Ricotta Cream
and Fruit Salsa

Honey-Ginger Peach Salsa

Makes about 3 cups

This dessert salsa is good spooned over ice cream, used as a filling in Sopapillas (page 141), or in Cookie Cups with Ricotta Cream (page 142). Or use it as the flavoring in homemade ice cream (page 140). You can substitute nectarines for the peaches if you wish.

INGREDIENTS

3 cups ripe peaches, peeled, pitted and cut
    into ¼-inch dice
1 jalapeño chile, unseeded, minced
1 tsp minced fresh ginger
1 tbsp honey
2 tbsp fresh orange juice
½ tsp cinnamon

METHOD

► Combine all the ingredients. Let sit for at least 30 minutes to allow the flavors to develop.

Tropical Dessert Salsa

Makes about 3 cups

This is a sweet salsa, with a touch of spiciness from the chili powder. Adjust the amount of chili powder depending on how hot you want the salsa and whether you are using commercial chili powder or ground dried chiles. For variety, add a tablespoon of chopped fresh mint. Like the other dessert salsas, it is good over or in ice cream (page 140), on Sopapillas (page 141) or in Cookie Cups with Ricotta Cream (page 142).

INGREDIENTS

1 mango, peeled, pitted and cut into ¼-inch dice

1 cup cantaloupe, cut into ¼-inch dice

1 cup fresh pineapple, cut into ¼-inch dice

1 tbsp brown sugar

about 1 tsp chili powder, to taste

1 tbsp fresh orange juice

1 tbsp fresh lime juice

METHOD

▶ Combine all the ingredients. Let sit for 30 minutes, then taste and adjust the seasonings.

Fruit Salsa Romanoff

138

Makes about 2 cups

This dessert salsa takes advantage of whatever seasonal fruits are available, but it traditionally includes at least some strawberries. Spoon it over ice cream or pound cake.

INGREDIENTS

¹/₄ to ¹/₃ cup sugar
¹/₃ cup fresh orange juice
2 tbsp orange liqueur or cognac (optional)
2 cups sliced or diced fruit, including at
*   least ¹/₂ cup strawberries, and your choice*
*   of peaches, plums, nectarines, apricots,*
*   cherries, seedless grapes, raspberries, or*
*   other fruit*

METHOD

▶ Mix together the sugar, orange juice and liqueur, adjusting the amount of sugar according to the sweetness of the fruit. Put the fruit in a bowl, pour the marinade over it and stir gently. Chill for at least 1 hour, stirring occasionally.

Banana Salsa

Makes enough salsa for 4 to 6 servings of ice cream

Okay, so maybe this is cheating a little. It's called Banana Salsa because the bananas are chopped and cooked with seasonings, but it's really a sort of chopped Bananas Foster, served over ice cream. Nevertheless, when the result is this delicious, who's going to quibble over a name?

INGREDIENTS

vanilla ice cream
3 tbsp butter
3 tbsp brown sugar
1/2 tsp cinnamon
3 tbsp rum, orange liqueur or orange juice
2 medium bananas, ripe but still firm, peeled and diced

METHOD

▶ Have someone spoon the ice cream into serving dishes while you are preparing the Banana Salsa, as it cooks quickly.

▶ Melt the butter over low heat in a medium skillet. Stir in the brown sugar and cinnamon until dissolved. Add the rum, liqueur or orange juice and stir for about 30 seconds. Add the bananas, cook for about 1 minute, until the bananas have softened slightly. Spoon over the ice cream.

Salsa Ice Cream

Makes about 2 quarts

If you have an ice-cream maker, you can use the salsas in this chapter in homemade ice cream. If you use Honey-Ginger Peach Salsa, you may want to add 2 more unseeded jalapeños, since the cream muffles their heat.

INGREDIENTS

1 cup heavy cream
2 cups whole milk
2 egg yolks
¾ cup sugar
2 cups dessert salsa

METHOD

▶ In a medium saucepan, combine the cream and milk and bring to a boil. Remove from the heat and let cool for 10 minutes. In a bowl, beat the egg yolks until they are frothy. Add the sugar and beat for 1 minute. Add a little of the warm milk to the eggs, to raise their temperature gradually without cooking them. Whisk the mixture. Add a little more warm milk, whisking, then gradually mix in the rest of the milk.

▶ Pour the egg-milk mixture into a saucepan and cook over low heat until the custard thickens slightly but does not come to a boil. Remove from the heat, cool, then chill for at least 30 minutes.

▶ Mix the custard with the salsa, then transfer to an ice-cream maker and freeze according to the manufacturer's instructions.

140

Sopapillas

Makes about 20 sopapillas

Sopapillas, little pillows of deep-fried pastry dough, are traditionally served with honey, or sprinkled with cinnamon and confectioner's sugar. For a new twist, try stuffing them with a dessert salsa.

INGREDIENTS

2 cups all-purpose flour
2 tsp baking powder
¹/₂ tsp salt
3 tbsp solid shortening
vegetable oil for frying
ground cinnamon
confectioner's sugar
1¹/₂ cups dessert salsa of choice

METHOD

▶ Mix the flour, baking powder and salt together in a bowl. Cut the shortening into the flour mixture until it resembles fine crumbs. Add ¾ cup water and knead until it forms a stiff dough, a little moister and more elastic than pie crust dough. Wrap in plastic and let rest for about 30 minutes.

▶ On a floured board, roll out half the dough to a thickness of ¹/₈ inch. Cut out 3-inch squares. Gather up the scraps, combine with the remaining dough, and repeat.

▶ Pour vegetable oil into a deep skillet to a depth of 1 to 2 inches. Heat to 375°F. The temperature is important because if it is too cold, the sopapillas will be greasy; if it is too hot, the outside of the sopapillas will brown before the inside is cooked. Put a few squares of dough in the hot oil. They should not touch. Cook until puffy and golden brown, turning once, about 1 minute a side. Remove and drain on paper towels. Let the oil return to 375°F between batches.

▶ Dust the sopapillas with cinnamon and confectioner's sugar. Cut a slit along one edge and stuff with a spoonful of dessert salsa.

141

Cookie Cups with Ricotta Cream and Fruit Salsa

Makes 12 cups, 2 per serving

These desserts are light and elegant. Although the individual components can be made early in the day, the salsa should not be added until just before serving time.

INGREDIENTS FOR COOKIE CUPS

1/2 cup toasted pine nuts (see note below)
3 tbsp butter at room temperature
1/3 cup sugar
1/2 tsp vanilla extract
3 egg whites
1/4 tsp cinnamon
1/8 tsp salt
5 tbsp all-purpose flour
Ricotta Cream (recipe follows)
about 1 cup of dessert fruit salsa of your choice

METHOD

▶ Preheat the oven to 375°F. Grind the roasted pine nuts to crumbs in a food processor, taking care not to let them turn to paste. Set aside.

▶ Line 2 cookie sheets with parchment or wax paper. Have ready an ungreased 12-cup muffin pan.

▶ Cream the butter, sugar and vanilla extract. Add the egg whites, cinnamon and salt, and beat until the mixture is smooth. Add the ground pine nuts and the flour, and mix by hand until smooth once more.

▶ Drop tablespoonfuls of the batter onto the prepared cookie sheets, 4 inches apart. With a rubber spatula, spread the batter into thin, 3-inch circles. Bake until the cookies are firm and have just started to brown around the edges, about 7 minutes. Because you have to work fast with the baked cookies, it is best to bake only one sheet at a time.

▶ As soon as the cookies are done, remove them from the oven. With a wide metal spatula, carefully remove each warm cookie from the sheet, and gently press it into a muffin cup so that it forms a cup. The crimped edges do not need to be uniform. Work quickly so that you get all the cookies into the muffin pan while they are still warm, otherwise, they will crack. Repeat with the second sheet of cookies. Let the cookies cool in the muffin pan. (*Note:* If it is a humid day, the cookies will not get crisp, so leave them in the muffin pan until serving time.)

▶ Divide the Ricotta Cream among the Cookie Cups. This is best done no more than 2 hours before serving time, so that the cookies do not become soggy. Immediately before serving, top each cup with a tablespoon or so of fruit salsa.

INGREDIENTS FOR RICOTTA CREAM

1/2 cup whipping cream
1/2 tsp vanilla extract
1/2 cup ricotta cheese
1/2 cup powdered sugar

METHOD

▶ Beat the whipping cream with the vanilla extract until soft peaks form. In another bowl, beat together the ricotta cheese and powdered sugar. Fold in the whipped cream. Refrigerate until ready to use.

To toast pine nuts: Spread them in a single layer on a baking sheet. Bake at 350°F for 5 to 10 minutes until they are golden brown. Watch pine nuts carefully as they burn very quickly.

142

INDEX